I0023945

Richard Mansfield

Blown Away

A Nonsensical Narrative Without Rhyme or Reason

Richard Mansfield

Blown Away
A Nonsensical Narrative Without Rhyme or Reason

ISBN/EAN: 9783744673518

Printed in Europe, USA, Canada, Australia, Japan

Cover: Foto ©Thomas Meinert / pixelio.de

More available books at **www.hansebooks.com**

BEATRICE AND JESSIE.

BLOWN
AWAY

A NONSENSICAL
NARRATIVE · WITHOUT
Rhyme · or · Reason
related · by
RICHARD · MANSFIELD

and

Published·by·L.C.PAGE·and·COMPANY
BOSTON ·   · 1897

Copyright, 1897

By L. C. Page & Company

(INCORPORATED)

———

Entered at Stationers' Hall, London

Colonial Press :

Electrotyped and Printed by C. H. Simonds & Co.
Boston, Mass., U. S. A.

PREFACE.

SHOULD any person labor under the impression that any beast or thing described in this volume is intended for a caricature of him, he is in error. This book contains no sarcasm, satire, or cynicism. It was written as a purely childish and innocent pastime. It hides no sting. It was never intended for publication. There exists no adequate reason why it should have been published. It relates no story. It has no point, policy, or purpose. If the author harbored any design, it was to entertain some young people during a lengthy journey. It was then tossed aside and forgotten. It should *not* have been disturbed. Alas! it cropped up one day by the seashore, — a rainy day. The author read these pages to a number of small boys who could not escape. The smallest and least intelligent boy was amused. He bore out the promise of his childhood by becoming a publisher. He trailed the man who had corralled him that rainy day. His object was to wreak a long-delayed vengeance by publishing this book. He accomplished his fell purpose by bribing the author. Nothing remains but to pity the author, and to execrate the publishers.

The author's affection for his wife is his reason for not dedicating these pages TO HER.

THE AUTHOR.

Sept. 11, 1897.

ILLUSTRATIONS

ILLUSTRATIONS.

BLOWN AWAY.

BLOWN AWAY.

THE rain fell in torrents; the trees in the garden were bowing beneath it, — the lawn and the flower beds, our special pride, were all sodden. Most of the bright blossoms lay beaten down, draggled and flat, upon the dark soil. The gravel paths were formidable rivers. We stood dismally by the window and conversed in whispers. There was born an apprehension in our minds as to the likelihood of a repetition of the Great Flood; we were carefully casting up the sum of our virtues with a view to the possibility of a miraculous deliverance. The cat in the kitchen, our dearest bull-terrier, "Rags," and the much-shared pony (black, with an innocent white face), were by acclamation voted honorary members of the prospective ark.

The Picnic party so long looked forward to was postponed.

We had stolen to the window in our white gowns many times the past night to investigate the sky.

We were as miserable as disappointed children may be. Our particular friends and neighbors, Beatrice and Jessie, not bad sort of girls as girls go, though wofully addicted to chocolate caramels, were the participants of our sorrow. They had been hurried in from next door under a large umbrella. Their white dresses and blue silk ribbons had painfully reminded us of our loss, and we had mingled our tears. We had been specially indulged at tea: Nurse Anne had vainly spread brown sugar on our bread and butter. Even raspberry jam, hitherto an unfailing panacea, had proved stale, flat, and unprofitable.

Trickle, trickle, trickle, drip, drip, drip, said the rain. Every now and then the wind wailed in the chimney. Beatrice was perceptibly alarmed; there was no mistaking the corners of her mouth. I had caught a fly and was torturing it. At last our old nurse removed her spectacles, wiped them carefully, placed them in her work-basket, and looked at us meaningly. We fled to her.

The fly crawled up the window-pane slowly, minus a leg, — the girls squatted on the floor. There were three of them: Beatrice, Jessie, and my small black-haired sister. My dignity could fall to no such condescension, — I perched in the window-seat and sat on my legs to keep them still. Nurse Anne then commenced her story:

In the valley of Palisada, not far from the broad and rapid Omagama River, there lived, not many years ago, a widow who was the mother of forty daughters. Of these forty beautiful children, none of whom were as yet out of their teens, only two concern us, and these not so much on account of the deeds they accomplished as because of the startling adventures which befell them, and which I shall proceed to relate without further *hors d'œuvres* or preamble.

These two children were named Beatrice and Jessie. They were not both called Beatrice and Jessie; but one was Beatrice, and the other was Jessie, and I shall refrain at the present moment from telling you which was which.

Nobody ever knew why the modest widow called Beatrice and Jessie such names, and I fear it will remain forever a secret buried in the lady's bosom. But what does it matter? A rose by any other name would smell as sweet, and so no doubt would, — but let that pass.

It was at no particular time, — or if it was, I am unable to recollect it, — and at no particular period of the year, that our story opens. (It is best to be careful and never commit yourself to any direct statement which, later on, may be used by your enemy as a handle to something or other to hit you with. The world being very wicked, you cannot do better than to keep out of it.)

Beatrice and Jessie, — Jessie would be very much annoyed if she knew that I had placed Beatrice first, because she thinks it very foolish to place the horse before the cart, when the cart is so much the larger of the two, that is if you count the horse one and the cart too, — and you must be sure to spell too, T-O-O, or you will get mixed up and make the cart and horse three, when it is really only two, unless you take off the wheels, in which case it would be useless, and the horse wouldn't fool with it.

Beatrice and Jessie were eating their breakfast, after a big ball which they had attended without their mother's permission, and were trying to tell her everything about it without betraying the fact that they had been there, and Beatrice was doing her best to go to sleep in her coffee-cup, when the door was suddenly opened by a cyclone which tore away the poor children who had been hanging on to Jessie's words, and left them without any support whatever. And herein was emphasized the sinfulness of fibbing, for if Jessie's statements had been substantial,

the thirty-eight sisters who were hanging
on her words would all have been saved.

But 'tis too late to change matters now.
The entire family, including the mother,
was scattered to the four winds, and per-

haps even more.   The thirty-eight and the
bereaved mother were never discovered,
although a number of expeditions were
sent out to search for them, and other
expeditions had to be forwarded to find
the first expedition, and so on.   But let

that pass. Let us follow the fortunes, — which is absurd, for neither of them had a penny, — of Beatrice and Jessie, or *vice versa*.

The cyclone lifted both of them and car-

ried them an enormous distance through the air. Fortunate were they that it did not carry them through the mud, or through the ink, or through fat, or many things I could name but will not. No, it carried them through the air, and finally

dropped them on a dry bank and left them
there on deposit.

The time had now come for Jessie to
polish her fingers and for Beatrice to
wash her hair, and as the sun was out,
shining beautifully, they concluded to
have their boots blacked; and after this
they were ready for visitors.

It was very disagreeable, of course, to
have to sit upon a bank with all the windows open, and as there was no door, it
wouldn't shut, and no door-mat, or anti-
macassar, or even anybody to answer the
door-bell or bring up the cards on a silver
salver, or call out the names of the visitors,
when they could see as plain, or even
plainer, than a pikestaff, or a broomstick,
who everybody was the moment they
came in or went out.

Jessie was pinning herself together
nicely, and Beatrice was reading a number of books every minute, when the nearest rat came to see them.

This rat had a very long tale, which they
listened to with great attention. The rat's

tale, in partibus or in omnibus, — for a rat
cannot afford a brougham, — follows, for
it would have been the height — or depth
— of ill manners for the tale to have pre-
ceded the rat; and, indeed, nothing is
more annoying, when you make a call,

than to find that your favorite tale has
arrived there before you.

The rat explained that he had not
called from curiosity, but as a politeness;
and seeing them so unprotected on a
bank, without even a watchman or a
safe, he felt it his duty as an old rat
to give them a little useful information
and advice.

Right here the rat was interrupted by a

raven who had entered unobserved, and who, having taken a chair on a bough, remarked: "Pardon me, young ladies, but I should not place too much credence in anything that old rat says; he is an exceedingly wily fellow, and known to be not overscrupulous."

At this, the rat seemed to be somewhat annoyed, and, putting up his eyeglass with a very supercilious manner, observed: " I have always regretted that that thing has wings; were it not for them I should be able to gnaw him. Please ignore him."

"Those who do," retorted the raven, "are a l w a y s sorry, as I can prove to you by referring to several historical works I have in my library at home. I am a first-class clairvoyant. I live up four flights,

but my charges are not high; call if you
please, here's my card, — Caw, Caw."
And several members of the Raven
family who had assembled joined in the
chorus.

"Listen to me," said the rat, "and pay
no attention to these niggers, —

> "There is a boarding-house,
> Far, far away."

"Oh, I've heard that," said Jessie, and
"So have I!" echoed Beatrice, "I know it
by heart."

"I'm sorry," said the rat, "I didn't in-
tend to quote; but I can't help it, I'm so
learned. I've been through so many books.
However, it's a fact, — there is, — and you
must try to find it, for I have discovered
that your happiness, and the happiness of
others, lies entirely in that direction. You
will excuse me, I am sure, but I feel the
poetical vein in me is bursting, — so if you
don't mind:

> "There, in a boarding-house
> Not over airy,

For the last hundred years
    Has resided a fairy.
This powerful woman,
    With tyrannical rule,
Feeds a score of her boarders
    On sulphur and gruel.
If anything enters
    This ill-omened house,
It can't get away, —
    Not even a mouse.
To look at the fairy
    Will give you a chill, —
Just look at her talons,
    And look at her bill!
She needs not to scratch
    Or to hurt you a jot, —
You look at her bill,
    And fall dead on the spot.
To enter her kingdom
    The trials are most awful!
There are cats by the legion,
    And smells by the jawful."

"I don't like that poem," said Jessie.

"No," said Beatrice, "and I don't think the metre is right."

"There is no metre in the boarding-house," placidly replied the rat; "and it isn't fair to expect it in the poem. You'll have to hear it all, and it isn't polite to interrupt a recitation at a party."

"Oh, Lor!" said the raven, "I wish I were dead."

"So do I," said the rat.

"Let's have it over," said Jessie, trying to look polite.

"Very well," remarked the rat, "but don't disturb me again, or I am likely to cry.

> "In the home of this fairy,
>   Quite under her thumb,
>   Lives a beautiful prince —

"There, I've forgotten it, — that comes of interrupting me. What rhymes with thumb? — quick, silly."

"Gum," said Jessie.

"No, it isn't gum, — stick to it; try again," said the rat.

"Mum?" said the raven.

"Idiot," said the rat.

"Dumb?" said Beatrice.

" Go up top," said the rat.

" In the house of the fairy,
  Quite under her thumb,
Lives a beautiful prince,
  Who's deaf, blind and dumb."

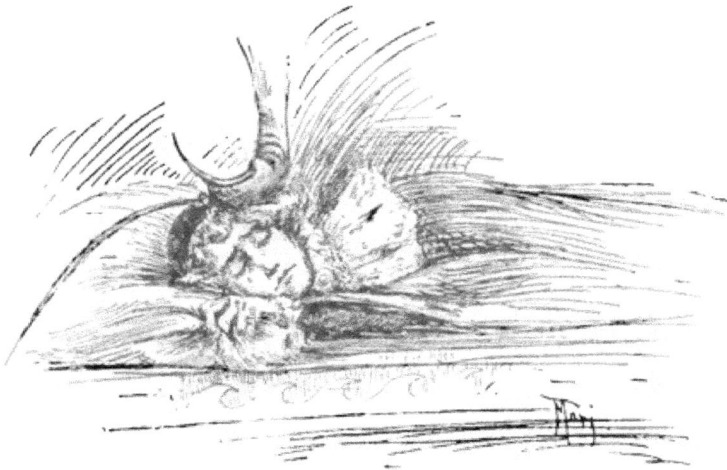

" How very sad," said Beatrice. " Can't
anything be done about it ? "

" You shall hear," answered the rat.

" This beautiful prince
  Is slave to the fairy,
Who makes him churn butter
  All day in the dairy ;

And as she is Irish,
  She has all the Pats
Wrapped up in fine linen,
  And packed up in vats."

"It's rot," said the raven.

"Who wrote it?" said Beatrice.

"It isn't my fault," said the rat. "It's by the bard."

"It's by the yard," said the raven.

"Shakespeare?" asked Jessie.

"I think so," said the rat.

"It must be very fine," said Beatrice, "only I didn't, perhaps, quite understand it at first. I'd like to read it carefully."

"Listen," said the rat, "I haven't done yet."

The raven fell off his chair, and the rat nearly killed it before it could get up again.

"This is awful!" said Beatrice.

"It was a contretemps," said the rat.

"I'm glad it has such a nice French name," said the raven. "It makes me feel better, and as long as I know that I am in polite society, I don't mind what happens."

"Be quiet," said the raven's aunt, "and listen to the recitation."

"Yes, aunt," said the raven.

"To rescue the prince
    From the wicked one's clutches,
Has been tried by all nations
    From Chinese to Dutches."

"What's Dutches?" inquired Jessie.

"I'm sorry you're so ignorant," exclaimed the rat. "They live in Holland."

"Then I hope they'll stay there," said the raven's aunt, who was taking a cup of tea. "I'm sure we don't want them here, —we're overpopulated."

"Who's interrupting now?" asked the raven.

"Don't be rude," said his aunt, "or I'll cut you off with a penny, and I know I'm going to die soon."

"In that case," said the raven, "I'll show you every attention."

" This is the worst party I've ever been
to," said the rat.

> " Who wins the fair prince
> His fortune and name,
> Must be fair without beauty,
> And great without fame."

" That's like me," said Jessie.
" I don't fancy it a bit," said Beatrice.
" I can't help that," said the rat; " I
didn't do it.

> " She must enter the house, —
> Eluding the fairy, —
> And discover the prince
> Alone in the dairy.

> " She must kiss both his eyes,
> His lips and his ears,
> And sit down by his side,
> And call for two beers.

> " Then, when the witch enters
> To serve the zwei lager,
> Then — then —

" It's no use," said the rat, taking his
hat and cane. " I shall have to wish you

a very good morning ; you can't expect me to find a rhyme for lager, — it's asking altogether too much, and I've overexerted myself and feel faint. I'm very nervous and tired, so you'll have to excuse me."

" Oh, do finish the poem," said Beatrice.

" Impossible," answered the rat. " You'll have to find out the remainder for yourselves. However, as you've been as polite as your limited education will permit, I will assist you a little, if you wish to rescue the prince. You must keep along Piccadilly until you come to Mount Arrowroot. Ask at the Ark for further directions, and then turn to the left and keep straight, if you can. If Miss Jessie will give me the scissors, I should feel obliged,— I want to trim my whiskers,— and in exchange you may call upon us whenever you need assistance. Just shout as loud as you can, and I'm sure to hear you."

" Whom shall we call for ? " asked Beatrice.

" Rats ! if you please," said the rat, and bowing politely to the ladies, and with a haughty stare at the raven, he walked swiftly in the direction of the Holborn Viaduct.

" I don't think," observed Beatrice, " that our first party was a great success."

" Well," Jessie replied, " we didn't really invite anybody, you know, but the rat was very polite to recite."

" I don't know," said Beatrice. " I don't like people who put themselves forward, and he never asked me to sing. Let's go out and look for the Ark and do some shopping. Who'll dress first ? "

" I will," said Jessie, " because I can jump into my clothes."

" Very well," said Beatrice, " you jump, and I'll clean up the tea things."

Jessie entered the hollow tree which they used as a dressing-room, and broke the jumping record, and then Beatrice hurried in to dress. It was quite dark inside, and if it had not been for the owl, whose eyes served as lamps, Beatrice would not have been able to see at all.

" I don't suppose," said the owl, " while

Beatrice was brushing her stockings, "that it has occurred to you that you are intruding?"

"No," said Beatrice, "am I?"

"Well, it isn't customary, you know, for people to walk into other people's rooms in this way, — especially when they're asleep. Are *you* going to sit up all day, may I ask? Would you mind turning me over? I'm tired of lying on this side."

"Are you going to sleep all day?" asked Beatrice, after she had complied with the owl's request.

"Of course, ninny," said the owl. "You don't expect me to sit up, do you? People who stay up all day are silly; it hurts the eyes."

"I didn't think of that," said Beatrice.

"Of course not," said the owl, "you should think a great deal more, and talk less."

"Could you lend me a looking-glass?" said Beatrice.

"What for?" said the owl.

" To see myself," said Beatrice.

" What for? " said the owl.

" To see myself," said Beatrice.

" Don't get angry," said the owl. " What for?"

" To see myself," said Beatrice.

" You've said that before," said the owl, "and it's stupid, — if you know what you look like you needn't see yourself. I know what I look like, and I don't want to see myself. If you don't know what you look like, it's time you did. Would you mind turning me over? I'm tired of lying on this side."

" It's silly to talk," continued the owl, when Beatrice had turned her over and smoothed the pillows and tucked the bed-clothes in around her toes. " It's silly to talk when you can think. By the way, if I wanted to be disagreeable, I should let you know that your dress is open at the back."

" Oh!" said Beatrice.

" Don't say 'Oh!'" said the owl, "it's silly; why say 'Oh?' — You might as

well say A, or B, or C, or any other letter
of the alphabet. But perhaps you only
know one?"

"I know them all," said Beatrice.

"I don't believe you do," said the owl.
"What comes after X Y Z?"

"What does?" said Beatrice.

"Nothing," said the owl,—"would you
mind turning me over? I'm tired of lying
on this side. After all, I'm not at all sure
that I shall let you know that your dress
is open at the back. One always makes
enemies that way. I'll let somebody else
tell you, and you won't dislike *me*. Are
you coming home to breakfast, may I ask?
and do you expect me to wait for you? I
hate waiting for breakfast, it always makes
me feel so faint. If you are going now,
would you mind turning me over? I'm
tired of lying on this side."

Beatrice had on her muff and her fur-
lined cloak and new goloshes and a fur
cap, and lots of other things that cost a
great deal of money.

The coachman touched his hat,—he

"'IF YOU ARE GOING NOW, WOULD YOU MIND
TURNING ME OVER?'"

didn't dare to grab it, because his hat was so very fine, with a cockade stuck in it, and polished so highly that you could see your face in it, if you put it on.

The footman opened the door most politely for Beatrice to enter the carriage; for he was a considerate man, and didn't want her to climb in through the window, or even open the door for herself, which would have been much worse.

The carriage was lined inside, throughout, with pale pink satin, and the horses had their tails tied up with pink ribbons. The coachman and footman wore big bouquets of pink flowers glued on to the front of their coats, and the rosettes in the horses' ears were pink, and Beatrice had a pink satin dress with a long train to it.

"I'm sorry," said Beatrice, after she had sat down and piled her dress up all about her, and put some of it out of the window and asked the footman to take great care of it until she needed it; "I'm sorry," said Beatrice, "that I put on my goloshes. I sha'n't know where to leave them when I reach the palace."

All this time the carriage was standing still, but the horses were pawing the ground so hard that it seemed as if they were really going quite fast.

"Why don't you move on?" said Beatrice.

"Just what I was going to say," said the policeman.

"You didn't say so," said the footman; "you only told me to hold your dress."

"No," said the coachman; "you didn't say so. If you had said so, it would have been all different. It's hard work sitting here and holding the horses. I've a good mind to get off and leave them."

"Oh, please don't," said Beatrice. "I want to go to the palace."

"Very well," said the coachman, "but don't let it happen again; and I am not at all sure that I can go there now. Get up!"

"What for?" said Beatrice.

"I wasn't speaking to you," said the

coachman. " Don't interfere, or I can't drive."

" Oh ! " cried Beatrice.

" What is it now ? " said the coachman.

" I've forgotten Jessie," said Beatrice.

" Well, I can't help that," replied the coachman ; " you'll have to learn it again and say it to-morrow."

" You'll have to drive to Blanchard's and call for her."

" I sha'n't," said the coachman. " I'll drive the horses there, but I won't call for her, — you'll have to do that yourself. I'm hoarse to-day, and I'm going to address a political meeting this evening."

" Very well," said Beatrice.

" I don't think so," said the coachman.

Jessie was waiting at Blanchard's, and in order to kill time, and abbreviate her own existence, she had eaten a strawberry ice, a chocolate ice, a lemon ice, two almond cakes, and had drank three glasses of lemonade and one of cream.

Jessie had on her yellow silk dress trimmed with black lace and parsley, and

she held in her hand a large bouquet,
which had been sent to her by an anony-
mous admirer, whose name was written in
a fine, bold hand upon a card which was
attached to the bouquet by a wire.

Jessie climbed into the carriage, which
joined a long line of other vehicles full
of beautiful girls on their way to the
palace.

The Queen was considerably flustered
that so many people should come to spend
the evening with her unexpectedly.

" I don't like surprise parties," said the
Queen, " unless I am told about them be-
forehand, so as to have things ready.   May
I inquire whether you have brought anything ? "

Jessie held up a bath bun and Beatrice
an Aberneathy biscuit.

" Every little helps," said the Queen,
and everybody applauded vigorously, because everything the Queen said was reported to be very wise.

" Each girl must eat what she has
brought with her," said the Queen, and

"'I DON'T LIKE SURPRISE PARTIES.'"

all the girls tried to applaud again, but
some of them couldn't, and cried bitterly.

"It's no use crying," said the Queen,
folding her pocket-handkerchief carefully,
"and you can swap things if you want to."

"Who will give me
a raspberry tart for
a bath bun?" said
Jessie.

"Nobody!" said
everybody.

"Greedies!" said
Jessie.

"I'll have no quar-
relling," said the
Queen. "Send for
the Poet Laureate;
he'll eat anything
that's left over."

"I can't," said the Poet Laureate; "I've
been dining out."

"Then," said the Queen, "you'll have
to sing a song, or guess who hit you."

"I'd rather sing," said the Poet Laureate.

"Very well," said the Queen, sadly.

" I'm going out now, and when I return,
you must have finished."

The poet took a new banjo from his
pocket, and having carefully blacked his
face with a boot-brush, and arranged
his feet in front of him, in order not to
make any mistakes in the metre, proceeded to chant the following ballad to
a simple accompaniment.

" Oh, that the stars in the Empyrean gleaming
 Were stirred by the thoughts of the men
  that behold,
 And the songs of the minstrel, when soulfully
  dreaming,
  Could quiver those spangles of silver and
   gold !

" Can ever the lover, who's longing and pining,
 Unbitter his wormword of sovereign woe ?
 Or the poison that filters through shimmer-
  ing lashes,
  Can it deaden the pain and then soften the
   blow ?

" I question, — Oh, answer ! you never need
  ponder, —
  Nay, — swiftly reply to the query I throw !

I pause and you ponder, — ah, why should
you wonder?
Can you deaden the pain and then soften
the blow?

" What is it that lingers and raises a spectre
That haunts me at night and embitters
the fray?
Is it some dreary phantom that hid in the
nectar?
The shadow of something I dined off to-
day?

" Or, is it the ghost of the long since forgotten,
That echoes the strain of a piteous refrain
By strumming the strings of a heart that is
sodden
With memories naught can engender again?

" You will-o'-the-wisp that I'd drown to im-
prison!
You glimmering hope that I'd kill to embrace!
You stars that are mocking a curtained horizon! —
Can I know of you naught but the gleam
of your face?

> " Did I cast myself down from a peak to an
>   endless,
>   Did I dive in the jaws of that dragon be-
>   low ? —
> Oh, answer me, phantom, — me, — hideously
>   friendless, —
>   Could you deaden the pain and then soften
>   the blow ? "

" I can't understand a word of it," said
Beatrice, as the Poet Laureate shut up
the banjo and put his feet back in his
pocket.

" Of course not," replied the poet. " I
should lose my head if you did."

" Well," said the Queen, "let's have
dinner."

" Please, ma'am," said the new servant-
girl, " the Minister of War is down-stairs,
and wants to see you."

" Tell him to come up," said the Queen ;
" and be sure he wipes his boots."

" While we are waiting," said the poet,
" perhaps you will like this better :

> " O bottlefly and bumblebee,
>   O centipede and humble flea,

O earwigs dear, and thrifty ants,
That often clamber up my — "

" That will do," said the Queen; " you
can go now."

The Poet Laureate put on his wreath,
took the best umbrella out
of the stand, and went
out into the yard
and laid down in his
barrel.

The Minister of
War was a very tall
man, with a big white
moustache tied up in
curl papers. He was
riddled with shot of
every size, and had
sabre wounds all over
him. He was dressed in
a red coat and blue trousers,
and had on a large bearskin hat, which,
in order to be really military, he was
obliged to keep on his head always, even
when he took his bath or went to bed.

His sword was tied to his waist by a leather strap, which was so long that he could leave the sword on the hall table and come up-stairs in the dining-room and sit down without unbuckling it. The Minister of War was very abrupt in his speech, as of course he had to be, or he would not have been Minister of War. After hitting his head three times against the mantel-shelf, to prove that he was not afraid of anything, he said:

"Your Majesty, there's a war coming."

"Dear me," said the Queen, "where is it coming from?"

"I don't know," said the Minister of War, taking the curl paper from one side of his moustache and reading it. "I don't know, and if I did, I shouldn't tell. You must ask the Minister for Foreign Affairs; but I think you ought to postpone dinner until after the war is over."

"Put off dinner!" said the Queen.

"I haven't put it on," said the cook.

"Very well," said the Queen, "I never said you had."

"I've been looking out of the window," remarked the Minister of War, "and I can't see it anywhere."

"See what?" asked the Queen.

"The war," said the Minister. "I'm afraid I've lost it. I'll have to resign."

"Very well," said the Queen, "it doesn't matter very much. I'm going to wash my dog, and you must all go home now."

Beatrice and Jessie walked a long time, until they got back to the hollow tree.

"You've been a sad while away," said the owl. "It's very inconsiderate, — the kettle has boiled over, — and would you mind turning me over? I'm tired of lying on this side. If you think you know how to cut bread and butter, we'll have tea; and I wouldn't mind a slice of toast and a little raspberry jam."

"We have got to go out soon," said Beatrice, "to find the Ark."

"Very well," replied the owl, "I think I'll get up. If you're going out now, as it will soon be dark, you had better cut down a couple of stars and take them with

you, — here are the scissors. Just cut the
strings, and you can tie them up again
when you come home. You won't need
them in the Ark, — that's lighted by elec-
tricity, although I remember the time very
well when Noah had only a couple of oil
lamps. The Ark was a pleasant place
then, but you won't find me there now, I
can tell you. Pass the jam!"

"I wish," said the mouse, "Jessie were
not so tidy, — it's uncharitable to be so
tidy. I'm the mother of a large family,
and how are we to live, if you don't drop
any crumbs? I'm waiting, do you hear?"

"I can't eat any more," said Beatrice,
"and I feel very sleepy."

"I hope," observed the mouse, "you
will have the common decency to give
us our dinner before you retire."

"It is a sufficient comment," said the
owl, sitting back in her chair, and com-
placently stirring her tea, "upon the slan-
der which has been propagated concerning
my mouse-eating propensities, to call attention to that rodent, domiciled as it is

with its offspring under my very roof.
But Public Opinion is gradually driving
me to desperation, and I shouldn't wonder if some day I actually did swallow
that mouse."

Upon hearing this, the mouse gave vent
to a series of heartrending cries: "Children!" she shrieked, "pack up everything
and call a van; we shall have to move this
very evening. We are in the abode of a
horrible ogress."

"Not so fast," said the owl, gobbling
the mouse; "you haven't paid for your
board, — and now I must go out and buy
mourning for her children." Thereupon,
the owl put on her bonnet, and, wishing
Beatrice and Jessie a very good evening,
went out with a basket over her arm.

Beatrice and Jessie were very much
shocked at the horrible crime which had
been committed before their very eyes,
but this didn't prevent them from feeling
very sleepy. In a room up-stairs they
found two very pretty birds' nests lined
with eider-down, and with quilted silk cov-

erlets and green silk curtains, and both of
them were very soon fast asleep.   Their
dreams were so beautiful that they were
never able to remember them, but they
woke up bright and early, more determined than ever to rescue the handsome
but afflicted prince who was imprisoned
by the boarding-house fairy.

Several robins in red waistcoats prepared the morning bath, after bringing
them a large cup of chocolate and some
delicious rusks.

Beatrice was about to step
into her bath, when a roach,
taking off his hat and bowing
quite politely, said:

"Excuse me, but I fancy you
are not aware that you are taking a very serious step."

"I don't think it's so serious,"
answered Beatrice, "and I must say it is
very rude of you to intrude."

"I live here," said the roach, "and my
manners are perfect, — in fact, I am called
the Ravishing Roach, M. D."

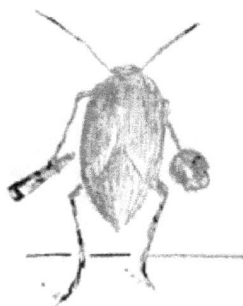

"Well, I shall take my bath just the same," answered Beatrice.

"In that case, I can only stand by and weep; but probably you do not know the havoc and destruction your thoughtless act will cause?"

"Tush," said Beatrice; "I think you are talking nonsense, and I must have my bath."

"You said that before," said the roach. "If you will have the kindness to look through this glass, you will perceive what you ought to have noticed long ago, and I fancy you will then change your mind; and I must say, without any intention of being discourteous, that it is quite time you did." With which, the roach made a profound bow, and offered Beatrice a magnifying-glass. "Look at your bath now," said the roach.

Beatrice looked through the magnifying-glass, and perceived, to her great astonishment, that the water was covered, here and there, with great countries, some of which were vast continents and others islands.

Everywhere she observed the greatest activity, — trains running in all directions, ships were sailing across oceans and into ports, steamers were plying to and fro, and in one country she could see a great war in progress, and could even hear the firing of cannon. A piece of Ivory Soap which she had thrown into the middle of an ocean was being settled with newly arrived colonists, and upon the sponge a large city was in course of construction. "What a wonderful thing," said Beatrice. "I might have destroyed all that, — but what am I to do? I must have my bath!"

"Well," said the roach, "I've been a good deal interested in that world ever since it was created this morning. If you'll give them another five hundred years, they'll be pretty well played out, and then you can go in and have your bath without really doing much harm."

"But I can't wait five hundred years for a bath," said Beatrice, "and I'm not sure I shall live so long."

" Oh," said the roach, " you'd call it five
minutes, but to them its five hundred
years. You see, you're so much bigger.
I hope you're not offended with me for
having interfered, — and would you oblige
me with my glass ? "

Beatrice was handing the roach the
glass, when Jessie entered the bathroom
and pushed poor Beatrice into the water.

" Oh, Jessie," cried Beatrice, " you don't
know what you've done. You've made
me destroy the world."

" It's no use crying over spilt milk,"
said the roach, fastening a piece of crêpe
to the handle of his front door. "Perhaps
you'll be a little more careful another time.
You'll excuse me now, I'm sure, but this is
my office hour, and I'm expecting a number of out-of-town patients. Good-morning."

" Please, Miss Beatrice and Miss Jessie,"
said the maid, " the laundress has brought
your linen, and it's all marked with a big
' O.' "

" Oh ! " said Beatrice.

" Yes, ' O,' " said the maid.

" Silly," said Beatrice, " it's an exclamation ! "

" It's an infraction," said the maid, who was very learned.

" What's to be done about it ? " asked Jessie.

" The laundress has marked all your linen with an ' O,' " repeated the maid.

" You said that before," said Beatrice.

" I thought I'd make it quite clear," said the maid ; " and what's more, she's marked them with thick ink."

" That isn't clear," said Beatrice. " Besides, you said ' it ' before, and now you say ' them.' "

" ' It ' is the linen, and ' them ' is the things," said the maid.

" *Are* the things," corrected Beatrice.

" They are," said the maid.

" Everything that is marked with an ' O ' is mine," said the owl.

" No, it's not." said Beatrice.

" Don't contradict," said the owl. " If you have any doubts about it, we had bet-

ter go before my friend, the Justice; he'll
decide. Come along." And herewith
the owl presented Beatrice and Jessie
with two pretty pieces of blue paper, on
which was printed a neat invitation to
come and see the judge at ten in the
morning.

Both the children were very pleased to
have so much notice taken of them, and,
having attired themselves in very pretty
dresses, they climbed into a tram-car,
which whirled them as quick as thought
to the beautiful palace where the Justice
gave a party every day.

Beatrice and Jessie were awestruck
when they entered the presence of the
functionary, who was a very fine, fat, elderly pig in an armchair. The Judge's
head was bald, which rendered his appearance very venerable, and he wore on
his nose a pair of gold eye-glasses. At
the corner of the Judge's desk a little pig
was stationed who was continually saying,
" Hats off!" " Hats off!"

Beatrice and Jessie, as soon as they

heard this, took off their hats and sat on them.

"You needn't have done that," said the Justice.

"Why not?" said Jessie.

"Silence in Court!" said the little pig.

"What do you want here?" said the Justice.

"Please —," said Beatrice.

"Silence in Court!" said the little pig.

"You mustn't say anything yourself," said the Justice.

"Who must say it?" asked Beatrice.

"Silence in Court!" said the little pig.

"Go ahead," said the Justice.

"Your Honor," said the cat, "I cannot proceed with this case if the sanctity of this Court is to be profaned by such levity on the part of the defendants."

"I shall have to fine them sixpence each," said the Judge, "and they must please pay it now."

"I've nothing less than half a crown," said Beatrice, "and if I change it, I'll spend it."

"You should have thought of that before," said the Judge; and he sent the little pig out to get the change.

"Little Pig," said the Judge, "purchase for me a pennyworth of roast chestnuts, two pennyworth of toffee, and a pennyworth of bull's eyes. Now then," continued the Judge, crossing his legs and closing his eyes, "let the case proceed."

"Please your Honor," said the tom-cat, who had climbed on to the back of the bench, and was snarling at Beatrice and Jessie, "these two persons have endeavored to rob my client, who is a hard-working, honest and thrifty widow."

"Is that true?" said the Judge.

"No," said Beatrice.

"Silence in Court!" said the little pig.

"They were about," said the cat, "to steal this linen, which belongs to my client and is marked with an 'O,' and I can, at any moment, if your Honor requires it, produce the laundress who marked the linen."

"It's ours!" said Jessie.

"Silence in Court!" said the little pig.

"Is it marked with an 'O'?" said the Judge.

"Yes, your Honor," said the cat.

"Have you anything to say," said the Judge, "why sentence should not be pronounced?"

"Please, Judge, —" said Beatrice.

"Silence in Court!" said the little pig.

"In that case," said the Justice, "the linen marked with an 'O' belongs to the owl, just as everything marked with a 'P' belongs to me, or everything marked with a 'C' belongs to the cat, — is there any one here who dare dispute that? Could anything be clearer, — anything plainer? In consideration of your extreme youth and the fact that this is your first offence, you may go. but you must never do it again."

"Do what?" said Beatrice.

"Silence in Court!" said the little pig; and Beatrice and Jessie were thrown out into the street.

"I don't like this at all," said Jessie; "we shall have to buy some sweets or I shall be very unhappy."

"Very well," said Beatrice. But just then a whirlwind happening to pass, they jumped in, and were left high and dry in a beautiful meadow, where innumerable bright flowers were blooming, where the lark was singing high above their heads in the blue sky, and where, by a transparent stream, a large red animal stood lazily fanning away the flies with a feather duster.

"Ask him the way to the 'Ark,'" said Jessie.

"Please —" said Beatrice.

"Excuse me," said the animal, "but I don't think we have been introduced, — at least I can't recollect having met you before."

"Perhaps not," said Beatrice.

"In that case," said the animal, "I must decline any further conversation."

"But I think I know you," hazarded Beatrice.

"Very likely," said the animal, "so do many people; but they are mostly mistaken. The party you are probably acquainted with, you may behold on the other side of the field. Good-morning."

Beatrice and Jessie turned about, and saw standing under a tree an animal that closely resembled the taciturn quadruped they had vainly endeavored to interrogate. On a branch above it was fastened a placard with the inscription, " Pull the bell."

" Where's the bell ? " said Jessie.

" Pull the tail," said the frog. who was trying experiments close by.

" I don't like to," said Beatrice.

" Oh, she won't mind," said the frog. " It's quite different over the way there. She's an aristocrat, and you have to bring an introduction, but anybody can call here. Have you money about you, may I ask ? "

" I've two shillings," said Beatrice.

" Well," said the frog, " that'll go a long way. You can buy buttermilk, or oleomargarine, or skim-milk, or tub-butter, and lots of things, — it's this one does the business. The other one, the genuine lady, is falling into innocuous desuetude. Look at her now chewing her cud and just giving milk, that's all. Why, it's absurd in these days of enterprise and progress. You must jump with the times,— I've often told her so. Milk ? absurd ! How are we going to feed the millions ? Look at all you children ; do you think,

—now I ask you,—do you think a cow
that can only produce milk and butter
and cream can feed all you children? Of
course not. Look at me; I'm full of enterprise and ideas and schemes, and you'll
hear from me presently, only keep your

ears open. Could you oblige me with a
pinch of snuff? Oh, well, never mind,
only I thought perhaps you knew that
snuff is coming into fashion again. I
jump with the times."

Beatrice pulled the animal's tail, and

was startled to hear a bell ring inside.
Instantly a door opened and a little old
man appeared.

"Plait-il?" said the man.

"I'm sorry to hear that," said Beatrice;
"I'll call another time."

"Non, non, non," said the little old man.
"Plait-il, français, — French, if you please.
Vat you vant, hein?"

"Oh, yes, I see," said Beatrice. "You
came out so suddenly, I didn't quite hear
what you said. Could you please tell us
the way to the Ark?"

"Ze Ark, — ah, ze Ark, ze mansion, ze
palais, ze château of ze great Monsieur
Noah? Oh, ah, you vant to zee heem,
hein?"

"Yes, please," said Jessie.

"Ah, ze ozer young lady, she also, she
vant to zee ze great Ark of ze great Noah?
Ees cet posseeble? You do not vant to
puy anyzeeng; you only vant to know ze
vay! Tonnerre! you have ze audace to
pull ze tail of ze bell to ask ze question.
It ees too mooch! I refer you to ze gen-

tleman himself, ze great Monsieur Noah of ze ark; he ees coming zees vay, behold heem! Bon jour, good-day, good-morning, good-evening, bon soir, au revoir, au plaisir, good-bye. I have ze plaisir to vish you goodnight."

"Can I be of any service to you," said a mellifluous voice at both their elbows.

Beatrice and Jessie turned, and instantly recognized the familiar figure of N o a h. He was dressed in precisely the same suit of clothes he had worn when they played with him in their ark at home. He also wore the same benevolent expression of countenance and the same rigid attitude; and he propelled himself by some mysterious manner upon the same green, round, flat pedestal which had proved his only ostensible means of support amid so many scenes of domestic vicissitude.

"Oh, it's Mr. Noah," said Beatrice and Jessie.

"Yes," replied the amiable figure, "it is indeed Noah, young ladies, — Noah himself. I flatter myself that my advertisements have not been in vain. I stand to-day the best-known figure in the show business of the world. It isn't every young lady that is privileged to see me, — that would be cheapening myself; but now that you've discovered me, you've found me, and here I am."

"Yes, there you are," said Beatrice and Jessie; and they were so delighted that they stared at him with their mouths wide open.

"That's true," said Noah, "but please shut your mouths; it's rude to open them so wide, and there is no telling what might fall into them. Always keep your mouths shut, if you wish to avoid danger. And now you would like to see the Ark? — it's a shilling each, please."

Beatrice gave Noah her two shillings, and Noah dropped them into his hat, which he always kept on his head because it was full of money — not his head, but his hat.

" This way," said Noah, very politely, but just then a terrible explosion knocked him down, and both Beatrice and Jessie were thrown to the ground.

"Oh, dear," said Beatrice, "what was that?"

" Please pick me up," said Noah, "and I will tell you."

Beatrice and Jessie tenderly placed Noah upright upon his pedestal.

" That explosion," said Noah, "was the frog. He has been experimenting for some time, trying to look like a cow. I warned him, but he wouldn't listen to me. He has just exploded with fatal results, — I think he has chipped a piece out of my trousers, and I shall have to be repanted in parts. Thus does the folly of others cause the suffering of somebody else. But let that pass. We will now go into the Ark, which, as you know, stands upon Mt. Arrowroot, — not the original Mt.

Arrowroot, — I have disposed of that in pieces, at a penny a piece, and some of it has been stolen by wicked sightseers, but still it's Mt. Arrowroot, — you can't take the name away, you know."

" Is it far from here ? " hazarded Jessie.

" It's on the tenth story," said Noah, " but there is an elevator, and a boy in uniform. Here we are." And Noah pointed proudly to a sign which read, " Take this elevator to the Ark, — keep to your right for the trains — go down the steps to the boat." " It's not too late to turn back, young ladies, if you're afraid. The animals have all been fed, — but still accidents will happen in the best regulated families."

" If you'll excuse us for a moment," said Beatrice, " we will hold a convention."

" Take your time," said Noah, politely.

Beatrice and Jessie sat down and talked rapidly for three hours, until the setting sun and the dead birds that lay all around them reminded them that the discussion had been lengthy, whereupon they rose simultaneously, and, with a deep courtesy, informed Noah that for ill or for woe, for better or for worse, they were prepared to face the animals in the Ark.

"But," said Noah, "you must promise not to talk to the animals too much. In fact, we don't allow ladies to talk to the animals at all, — it hurts them."

Beatrice and Jessie promised faithfully not to enter into conversation with any beast.

"In that case," said Noah, "I will trust you."

The boy in the elevator was very pleased to see Beatrice and Jessie. He spoke to them kindly and with much affability, and he further manifested his amiable disposition by a promise to eventually lend them a book he was then perusing.

After having been shot twice through the roof, and after two descents to the cellar, they finally arrived at their destination. Noah took Jessie by one hand and Beatrice by the other, or Beatrice by one

"BEATRICE AND JESSIE SAT DOWN AND TALKED RAPIDLY FOR THREE HOURS."

hand and Jessie by the other, I forget which, and walked with them to the Ark. Both Beatrice and Jessie were trembling with excitement.

" You must not tremble so," said Noah, "you are shaking the glue, and unsettling me for my work. It is only by preserving a stolid countenance, every autumn when sugar is cheap, that I am able to subdue my animals; and before you go in," continued Noah, " I'm sorry to say you will have to listen to a recitation,— it's part of my duty, and I must do it. I'm sorry, nobody ever likes it, but I *must*, and you can have refreshment afterwards."

Beatrice and Jessie, being obliging girls and accustomed to afternoon parties, smiled bitterly, and assented.

The usher conducted them to a front seat on the aisle, and Noah, having powdered his face and made some other necessary alterations in his dress, such as the theme of his recitation demanded, declaimed the following :

" Beware how you face the lion's maw,
    Beware the pussy's fiendish claw,
    Nor brave the squirrel's horrid roar.
                            Excelsior!

" Let not the dromedary's smile,
    Nor crocodiles with tears beguile ;
    Let not the chimpanzee or clown,
    Or horse that gallops up and down,
    Or bull that wallows in his gore,
    Or bees that hive their sugared store
    Which little girls like you adore.
                            Excelsior!

" Let not the donkey's bray convince,
    Or wolves and monkeys hash and mince ;
    Let not the cow or lowly swine
    The mole and hedgehog undermine,
    Nor other quadrupeds galore,
    Yea, ten or twelve or even more,
    That bide within my humble store.
                            Excelsior!

" This is no time to launch the Ark,
    Or stir the scaly, slumbering snark ;
    To shave the dog or shear the sheep,
    Or wake the weasel when asleep,

Or stay the chamois in his leap,
To call the dentist to the boar,
Or manicure your father Noah.
                    Excelsior!

" Lie still and hear the jungle breathe,
And watch the elephant on the heath,
The ducks and flies and myriad things,
And all the beasts that boast of wings.
And do not fool with tails with stings, —
The snakes and scorpions on the floor
Are not on speaking terms with Noah.
                    Excelsior!

" Look here and there and everywhere,
But take my warning and beware, —
Yea, look your fill at every beast,
Not this the more nor that the least
(The price is low and vast the feast), —
Yet, ah, beware, and do not jaw
The an-i-mals of father Noah!
                    Excelsior!"

" That's very nice," said Beatrice ; " only
I don't quite understand ' Excelsior.' What
does it mean ? "

Noah's eyebrows went up under his hat, and appeared after a while under his chin. " Excelsior," he said, " is etceteror, or so on and upwards. When you say excelsior, or etceteror, or so on and upwards, you leave a great deal to the imagination, which is always a fine thing in everything.

" And now," said Noah, spinning round rapidly on his base, " I will present you to the animals. There are fortunately a good many of the genuine ones still left. At first most of the original stock was on tour, but now the demand for the manufactured article, or fake, is so great that the old ones are falling into the sere and yellow leaf, which is the best I can afford, the price of flesh and hay being so high."

" Do the animals ever leave the Ark? " said Beatrice. " I thought they couldn't get out because the water was so high."

" The water rates are high," answered Noah, " but it isn't there the shoe pinches. Of course they travel. The Ark has been so much talked about that people desired

ALASKAN
GHIGANTICUM-PLETHORATHOREUS.

Do Not Feed
HIM PEANUTS

"'I HAVE TO MANUFACTURE BEASTS TO
SATISFY THE PEOPLE.'"

to see the animals, and I sent out several companies under the management of my boys, Shem, Ham, and Japhet. Perhaps you've seen some of them?"

" I've seen a circus," said Jessie.

" That's it," said Noah. " It's a circus, that's what it is, — but let that pass. Now the people are no longer satisfied with one head to a calf, or an ordinary face on a dog, or a snake of common proportions; I have to manufacture beasts to satisfy the people, and the real ones stay at home."

" Don't they get tired of it?" asked Beatrice.

" Tired? Bless you, no; we're a happy family. We play cards, and have dances and private theatricals, and read books and talk about one another. Perhaps, if you are very good and please them, you may be allowed to witness one of our talented entertainments. But walk in, walk in, and I'll introduce you, if you'll give me your names, which I think you forgot to tell me."

Beatrice and Jessie imparted the information, and, having carefully crossed a plank which was placed over the gutter, Noah rang the bell, a neat maid opened the door, Noah hung up his hat in the hall, and ushered them into the Ark.

"Whom have we here?" said the bear, walking up to Noah and digging him in the ribs. "Who did you say, eh?"

"These young ladies," said Noah, "are Miss Beatrice and Miss Jessie. They have come to call."

"H'm," said the bear, "I don't like their looks. Sit down, if you can find a clean chair. We had a beastly bad dinner to-day, and I don't think you'll find us in a very good temper."

"Speak for yourself," said the jackal.

"Forage for yourself," said the bear.

"He's got a sore head," said the bull.

"He's got a thick head," said the bear.

"If you're going to have a game of repartee," said the elephant, who stood in a corner, "let me out."

"He always says that," said the bear.
"He can't get out; he's too big."

Just then a bird flew in through the
window, and, having carefully locked away
a little green branch in a drawer, sidled
up to Beatrice and Jessie, and said, "You
think I'm a dove, don't you? Well, I'm
not. I'm a pigeon. The dove was married long ago, and lives down Kensington
way."

"Aren't *you* the dove with the olive
branch?" said Beatrice.

"Everybody thinks I'm a dove," answered the bird, "but I'm not; I'm a
pigeon. A new olive branch every day
is too expensive, — the one I use is artificial, and I always lock it up in a drawer,
or some beast would eat it. I hide it
under my wing when I go out, and fly
back and pretend I've found it. I make
three trips a day. I always interest visitors. They think I'm a dove, but I'm not;
I'm a pigeon."

"If you're going to say that again,"
remarked the elephant, "let me out."

"He always says that," said the bear. "He can't get out; he's too big."

"My name's Jacob," said the jack-daw.

"Don't tell that bird anything," said the bear; "he'll repeat it."

"When is a door not a door?" asked the wild boar.

"The boar always asks riddles," said the bear.

"Give it up?" asked the boar.

"If you're going to ask riddles," said the elephant, "let me out."

"When it's a jackdaw," said the boar.

"I love domestic felicity," remarked the rabbit to the hare. "Meander with me in the plaisance."

"I'm henpecked, that's what I am," said the hare.

"No unpleasant reflections, if you please," said the hen, "or I'll hurl an egg at you."

"She's so old and tough," said the calf, "she lays hard-boiled eggs."

"It's not true," said the hen. "They're soft-boiled, — only three minutes."

"Oh, dear!" said the lion, yawning and emitting a fearful growl.

"Good gracious!" said the cat, "he's horribly out of tune, and we're so musical, — tune him, somebody."

"I'll not be tuned," said the lion. "I don't want to be tuned; I want to be amused."

"Very well," said the pig, "what do you say to supper?"

"Oh, if you're going to have supper," said the elephant, "let me out."

"Couldn't I eat these two young ladies, — pour passer le temps?" inquired the lion.

"Not for the world," said Noah. "It would kill my business. You can have amateur theatricals."

"Very well," said the lion, "but don't give the monkey a part."

"Am I scratched?" asked the monkey.

"You've scratched yourself," said the lion.

"If you're going to have private theatricals, let me out," said the elephant.

"He always says that," said the bear. "He can't get out."

"Who'll be leading lady?" said the bulldog.

"I," said the little deer; "they always like me."

"I am much better fitted for the part," said the cat. "I've a higher voice and more intelligence, and I'm accustomed to sit up late."

"This way," said Noah to Beatrice and Jessie. "The performance is about to commence, — all the fashionable people are already seated. This way, this way." And Noah conducted Beatrice and Jessie to two lovely seats lined with velvet.

In front of them sat the King of Jumbles and the Queen of Jumbles, and all

their court, composed of a number of old
ladies with feathers in their hair and diamonds and rubies sparkling on their bare
necks, and gentlemen in warming-pans
and dish covers on their torsos and coal-
scuttles on their heads so highly polished
that you could see your face in any one of
them.

The boxes were occupied by other
people, — kings and queens and princes,
— who chattered and ate ices, and exhibited themselves to the common people
free of charge.

Presently the bell in the steeple struck,
and it was quite a long time before it
could be persuaded to go on. Then
the orchestra began to make a variety
of noises, and the august personages
stuck cotton-wool in their ears in order
not to hear them, but when it played
all the national anthems at one and
the same time, so as not to offend any
reigning sovereign on earth, the people
up-stairs and the people down-stairs all
rose together and gave three cheers for

nobody in particular and everybody in general.

Beatrice and Jessie were glad to be able to gaze for half an hour at a beautifully painted curtain. There were swans in a lake, a gondola, a palace and trees, a greyhound, and a handsome gentleman in short trousers trimmed with lace and a hat edged with feathers, handing a lady in a long bath-gown down a staircase; but when presently the curtain rolled out of sight and they beheld a row of trees painted on paper on each side of the stage, and several other paper trees stuck about here and there, and some more trees painted on a large piece of paper at the back, with a lovely round moon that stood quite still and shone so brightly that it hurt their eyes to look at, they screamed with delight.

" If you do that again," said the monkey, whom the jealousy of his associates had compelled to act as usher, " I shall have to eject you! "

"Can't we scream?" asked Beatrice.

"Certainly not," replied the monkey. "You're disturbing the performance."

"It hasn't begun yet," said Beatrice.

"Yes, it has," answered the monkey, "it begins with the moon. Look at your programme; what does it say?"

"It says, 'Moon in the Forest,'" said Jessie, who could read with great rapidity.

"Well, that's it," affirmed the monkey; "that's the moon in the forest, and you mustn't disturb it."

"Very well," said Beatrice, "we won't; only we didn't know the moon was so touchy."

"It is," said the monkey; "I've known it to leave the stage and refuse to play, for a mere trifle."

"Quite right, too," said Jessie. "I wouldn't hold the moon for a trifle."

"If you don't keep still," threatened the monkey, "it will be my painful duty to eject you." And with this he walked up the aisle with great dignity, and hung by his tail from the balcony.

"If the usher doesn't stop this tomfool-

ery," remarked the cat, who had just made
her entrance upon the stage, " I shall not
act any more."

The cat being a great favorite, the audience applauded, and when silence had been
restored, she scattered some sand upon
the boards and danced. The monkey
untied his tail, and asked an elderly gentleman, who had fallen asleep, for his
ticket.

> " In this sylvan glade,"

said the cat, smiling, because she was out
of breath,

> " In this sylvan glade,
>   Where zephyrs chase the cow —

" Talking of cows," said the cat, " re-
minds me of the fact that I must have a
little milk. In the meanwhile, with your
kind permission, my understudy will un-
dertake my part at a moment's notice,
and I must request your very kind in-
dulgence for her. If I had given her any
time for preparation, she might have played

the part too well, and you will, therefore, comprehend that she is entitled to every consideration. Charity begins at home." And with several courtesies the pretty cat retired from the stage, followed by a burst of applause which lasted for some minutes.

" Whilst Miss Pussy prepares herself to play the rôle recently performed by Mlle. Tabbi," said the prompter, " I have the profound honor to present to you Mrs. Piggy Wiggy, the great manageress. Mrs. Piggy Wiggy, ladies and gentlemen," continued the prompter, whose left eye was bandaged with a scarlet pocket-hand-kerchief, " Mrs. Piggy Wiggy, ladies and gentlemen, eats everything. She is a heroine; she eats paper, ladies and gen-tlemen, and those among you who have ever eaten paper cannot fail to be aware of its tough and indigestive qualities! Ladies and gentlemen, it was the heroic determination upon the part of Mrs. Piggy Wiggy not to be outdone by her rival, Mrs. Nanny Goat, that led her, in the interests of art, — and I may say of science,

— to devour manuscripts, bricks, tin cans, old clothes, boots; and furthermore, ladies and gentlemen, fired by that generous zeal and by that noble emulation which has ever been the striking characteristic of the Piggy Wiggy family, she did not pause at such trifles. No, ladies and gentlemen, there is nothing that she does not *try* to eat, nothing that she cannot eat, nothing that she will not eat! In the self-sacrificing devotion to art and literature and science, Mrs. Piggy Wiggy, ladies and gentlemen, has become plethoric, and alas! ladies and gentlemen, there exists a fear that some day she may burst; but if she does" (and here the prompter rose to a fine height of patriotic enthusiasm), "if she does, she will burst in the interests of art and literature and science! Before introducing the great manageress," continued the prompter, in a confidential tone, "I have to say that Mrs. Piggy Wiggy is of an amiable disposition unless she be balked in her desire to eat something. I trust, therefore, you

MRS. PIGGY WIGGY.

will not excite Mrs. Piggy Wiggy by
refusing to permit her to eat anything
in the audience she may fancy. Beyond
this, ladies and gentlemen, you may de-
pend upon Mrs. Piggy Wiggy's amiable
disposition and good-will."

The prompter now retired, and returned
with the renowned Mrs. Piggy Wiggy, who
was costumed as " The Distressed Mother,"
and wore a miniature portrait of herself in
medallion upon her breast. It was evident to Beatrice and Jessie that, although
Mrs. Piggy Wiggy smiled, she was suffering great pain, from the manner in which
she laid her hand upon the vicinity of her
heart, and, moreover, she was so fat that
her neck had entirely disappeared. The
audience, greatly awed by the sight of
this beautiful Piggy Wiggy, forgot to
applaud, and Mrs. Piggy Wiggy, having
grunted very pleasantly, trotted gently out
of sight.

" You haven't noticed me," said the
camel, who had posed, shrouded in a
black cloak and a broad-brimmed hat,

behind a tree. " It proves how realistic I am. I am not supposed to be seen, but still you ought to have accorded me a reception when I entered."

The audience apologized, and the play progressed. The camel resumed his effective pose behind a tree.

Mlle. Pussy, covered with blushes, and a pale blue ribbon tied about her slender neck and a delicate azure bow decorating her tail, stepped diffidently to the foot-lights.

" This lady," said the prompter, "has been imported from France, and although her language is foreign, her gestures and grimaces are so cosmopolitan that she can easily be understood even by those who have never studied Ollendorf."

Pussy drew on a pair of long black

gloves, which nearly reached to her waist, and slowly closing one eye, she daintily placed a forefinger upon the other, and dealing the King of Jumbles a killing glance from the thus isolated and concentrated orb, she sang:

" Quand Villikins se promenait dans son jardin
        un matin,
    Il decouvrit La Belle Dinah étendue sur son
        chemin,
    Une tasse de soupe poisonnée froide dans sa
        main
    Et un billet-doux lisant qu'elle s'était suicidée
        bien.

" Le corpus rigide il l'embrassait mille fois ;
    D'être separé de sa Dinah il ne l'endurait pas ;
    Il avalait le reste de la soupe exécrable
    Et fut enterré de suite avec sa Dinah aimable.

" Entendez bien la morale de ma plainte :
    D'un amant vulgeur il se change donc en
        saint,
    Et pour toute demoiselle que se tue par
        amour,
    Qu'il meurt en martyr un jeune bel-homme
        toujours ! "

"Hand that down to me," said the schoolmaster, sternly, "and, after I have corrected the mistakes, you can stay in whilst the other pupils are enjoying their well-earned holiday, and write it out fifty times."

"If you'll let me try again," pleaded poor pussy, with tears in her eyes, "I think I can say it better."

"No," exclaimed the camel, "you can't go on forever,—it isn't fair; it's my turn next. My parents and all my friends are in the house, and I want them to hear me."

"It's a topical song," said pussy, sobbing bitterly, "and I can continue as long as I please."

"How's that?" asked the camel, appealing to the prompter.

"Out," said the prompter, and poor little Miss Pussy trotted disconsolately away.

The camel, who was suffering with lumps, came forward and picked up the thread of the forgotten plot.

" Don't touch that !" cried the prompter,
" or you'll bring down the curtain, — it isn't
time yet."

The camel retired, and resumed his

effective pose behind the tree. A long
prolonged roar of genuine applause now
shook the house.

" Toby or not a Toby," said the orang-
outang, sitting down and gazing medi-

tatively at a pot of beer, " Toby or not a Toby?"

" The orang-outang," spoke a sad, lone voice close to Beatrice, " is unable to play this part. This character has not been adequately interpreted since the year 1611, when a stout person undertook the rôle in England. This orang-outang is a common and repulsive beast, and is entirely incapable of comprehending the delicate distinction of a Toby that is a Toby, and a Toby that is not a Toby. Woe, — woe, — ha, ha!"

" Why do you say 'woe, — woe, — ha, ha'?" asked Beatrice.

" Why, why," said the sad, lone voice, " because — "

" Because what?" asked Beatrice.

" Simply because," answered the sad, lone voice. " If you shut your eyes, you can see what I see; if you open your eyes, you will see nothing."

" That's ridiculous," exclaimed Beatrice.

" Woe, woe, ha, ha!" spoke the sad, lone voice.

"Did you ever know any one so provoking? What does 'woe, woe, ha, ha' mean, and why do you say it?"

"Shall I tell you, — shall I? Shall I shatter your dolls, your hobby-horses, your flower-beds, — shall I?"

"You can't," said Beatrice.

"Can't? Can't? Do you mean cannot? Oh, how soon, how soon? Woe, woe, ha, ha, — I say it always, ever, forever, this day, next day, sometime, never. I say it because what is woe is laughable, and what is laughable is woe. 'Woe, woe, ha, ha' is everything, something, all things, nothing. It's the pyramids. It's the sphinx!"

"Are you aware," asked the monkey, "that you are disturbing the acting?"

The sad, lone voice fell from his seat to the floor, and writhed there in a paroxysm of laughter. His merriment rolled in waves beneath the seats, and chilled the feet of the audience. Shaking then the dust from his loose habiliments, and sweeping the grizzled locks from his pale and thoughtful

forehead: " Acting? Did you, did you
say acting? Did you ever hear *me?* Can
I sit here and realize what is sizzling, fiz-
zing, and whizzing within me, and then
be still? Woe, woe, ha, ha! Only me,
and nothing more! Little children, shall
I break out? Shall I unbud, flower, bloom?
Shall I? It is smoldering, — shall I fan
it and let it flame? Acting? Oh, let me
not laugh again. See! I rise, I am rising,
I have risen. Only me, and nothing more.

" Empty is the china bowl, — the spirit flown
        forever ;
    Let the bell toll, and pretty Poll remove the
        scraps of supper ;
    Nectarian pop, hast thou no drop left of thy
        luscious store ?
    And of thy cheer, dear bitter beer, is there,
        alas ! no more ?
    Come, let the final hic be hoc'd, the parting
        song be sung,
    A pæan for the happiest dead that ever died
        so young,
    And coffee black and call a hack, and charge
        it to the thirsty pack.
    So young, so young, so young."

"If you talk all the time," remarked Beatrice, gazing with her eyes wide open at the strange creature by her side, "how can I listen to the beautiful play?"

"Listen? oh, lor!" said the strange, sad voice. "Hear her! Listen? I shall die; I shall fade away; I shall disintegrate. Listen, oh, lor!" And the sad, elderly, lone voice sprang upon his chair and executed a fierce, wild, weird dance; but alas! having touched some hidden spring in the mechanism of the seat, it suddenly collapsed, and enclosed the fallen lone one in its treacherous grasp. Beatrice and Jessie flew to his assistance.

"Leave me," gasped the sad, lone voice;

"this torture is preferable to listening; leave me, and let my bleached and mangled bones be found—" But Beatrice and Jessie would hear no more, and dragged the old gentleman from his perilous situation.

"Once upon a time," said he, "when I was a little thing like you, a head of lettuce, a sprout, a bud, I *did* listen,—but now,—oh, children, is it in your tender hearts to scoff at my gray hairs?"

A heavy flood of tears choked his utterance, and flowed from the strange one's eyes. Taking off his watch and chain, removing his boots, his hat, his coat, and waistcoat, he carefully enclosed them in a neat brown paper parcel, which he despatched by a messenger boy to his home; then raising his sweet voice, he sang:

"Once upon an evening dreary, when I felt a little queerly,
   Over many a quaint and curious vintage of my precious store,

While I nodded, nearly napping, suddenly
    there came a tapping,
As of some one gently rapping, rapping at
    my chamber door.
' 'Tis the janitor,' I muttered, 'tapping at my
    chamber door.'
        Only it, and nothing more.

" Indistinctly I remember it was in the bleak
    December,
And some moons were casting shadows round
    about the swaying floor
As I waited for the morrow with a sort of
    sick'ning horror, —
For in vain I'd sought to borrow, borrow just
    a trifle more
From that rare and radiant angel whom we
    mortals call Old Claw, —
        Only that, and nothing more.

" Then again there fell a tapping, and a louder,
    louder rapping,
And at last a cannonading and bombarding of
    the door,
Till I threw my gown around me, and I
    asked what may that sound be?

It has a voice familiar which I think I've
 heard before.
And raging at the shadows, I anath'matized
 Old Claw !
  Only that, and plenty more.

" It was vain to seek to slumber or to shake
 off care and cumber
While the enemy was peering through the
 crevice of my door,
So on tiptoe I stole slyly, and I squirted
 some ink spryly
Through the keyhole in the eyehole of the
 phantom at my door ;
And the voice that swiftly sounded had a
 baleful, hateful roar,
  And, I greatly fear, it swore.

" Now the shadows they moved faster as I
 danced and pranced with laughter
At the picture I created in my fancy at the
 door ;
And, with mockish rev'rence bowing to the
 wind that flowed in soughing,
I bent my body double as I opened wide the
 door,

As I stood aside to welcome at my chamber
  drear Old Claw, —
    Only he, and what he wore.

" He popped in, and he hopped in, and he
  spluttered and he stuttered,
And the darkness of his figure seemed e'en
  blacker than before ;
And he mumbled, and he grumbled, and then
  he deftly tumbled
In a chair that I had placed with grave intention on the floor ;
And this article of comfort lacked a claw and
  nothing more, —
    Only this, and nothing more.

" Then hideous rose the laughter, and it shook
  the roof and rafter,
As the moonlight bathed the figure sprawling
  prone upon the floor.
There it squirmed in curious fashion like a
  crawfish in a passion,
Moving hither, thither, thither, hither, with
  its tentacles galore ;
And in vain I sought to flee them, but they
  sprang out more and more, —
    And they seemed to be fourscore.

" Now my joy was turned to sighing, and I
          well-nigh came to crying,
     For, exhausted, it had chased me to a cup-
          board by the door,
     And the hideous thing was crawling, and its
          sightless suckers mawling
     All my Lares and Penates, yea, the dearest
          of my store ;
     For each hairy creeper ended in a vicious
          beaklike paw, —
               Something kin to hand and claw.

" All   around   the   chamber   ranging,   it   was
          changing, changing, changing,
     Now to this thing, then to that thing, each
          more dreadful than before.
     Here a child's face sweetly hideous, there a
          woman's smile insidious,
     With a jaded, faded beauty, ah ! most pite-
          ously forlore !
     Then a thousand pleading faces, ever more
          and more and more.
               More and more for ever more.

" Yet, with one hand, groping blindly, I now
          sought to pat it kindly,

For my folly was egregious, but imagine
    what I saw :
To placate it, or to sate it, — or to excom-
    municate it, —
I would gladly pledge my honor, which is
    worth a moidore,
Or in any way to force it to the outside of
    my door, —
      Where I much prefer a bore.

" Since I failed with my caresses, I bethought
    me of addresses,
And with eloquence impassioned I uprose to
    take the floor ;
And my nice articulation with my best gesti-
    culation
I conjoined in an oration I proceeded to out-
    pour,
And the Octopus retreated and said, plead-
    ingly, ' No more,' —
      Only this, and nothing more.

" Still he boiled and coiled and fluttered, and
    he lived and thrived and uttered,
And I suddenly bethought me of the many
    songs of yore,

And that if I sang them quaintly, how soon
　　he would a saint be
Whose iniquities were squirming in that mass
　　upon the floor ;
And I sang, and sang them blithely, till he
　　writhed and cried, ' No more,' —
　　　　Only that and nothing more.

" Though his grasp was now much lighter, still
　　I feared it might grow tighter
On the many things of value that I treasured
　　in my store.
I perceived that he was numbing, though
　　whenever I ceased humming
He at once did look about him with the wis-
　　dom of before,
And I then determined briefly he must die
　　for ever more, —
　　　　Yes for ever, ever more.

" Now, because I am a sinner, I had once been
　　asked to dinner
By a gen'ral who was Rated, sar, some time
　　befaw de war.
I bethought me of his story, that was flaccid,
　　stale, and hoary,

Which the Octopus for sartain, sar, had never
　　heard befaw, —
And I told de gen'ral's story of de time befaw
　　de war.
　　　And I told it ever more.

" Yes, for ever, ever more, yes, for ever, ever,
　　ever, ever, ever, ever more."

" Will you be quiet!" said Beatrice.
" Never," answered the sad, lone voice,
and carolled :

" Oh, curse not the Bard if he fly to the Jayers,
　Where Blower lies, carelessly sneering at
　　Fame,
　He belongs to the worthy communion of
　　Stayers,
　And cannot break off at this stage of the
　　game.

" The tongue that now oscillates loose in the
　　liar,
　Must have swept a proud thrill thro' the re-
　　gions of Art
　And the lip that now echoes the song of the
　　mire,
　Might have hallowed his name in a parent's
　　fond heart."

"Oh, *do* keep still," implored Beatrice, diving deep down into her pocket, and extricating from its meshes a chocolate caramel, misshapen perhaps, and covered with a fuzzy growth, but still a caramel. " Take that, do," said the sweet girl, as the sad, lone voice manifested some reluctance to rob her of her treasure. " Do, I'm sure you'll feel better, — I always do."

The sad, lone voice accepted the caramel, popped it into his mouth, and under its soothing influence sank into a deep and refreshing slumber.

" I should like," remarked the lion, who had in the meanwhile appeared upon the stage in an Elizabethan costume, " I should like to have the lights turned on a little higher."

"The gas bill is too high," said Mrs. Piggy Wiggy from the wings ; " and moreover, this scene is played by moonlight to save the candles."

" That doesn't affect me," said the lion. " The moon is shining on my back, and the audience must see the expression of my face. I'm going to show them a new expression presently."

"Very well," said the prompter; "but you'll spoil the moon."

"If you do," said the elephant, "I'll take the moon away."

"All right," replied the lion. "I can do without it. What's the use of moons and things? I can do *without* them; I can do without anything. Expression's what you want!"

The audience gave three cheers, and the play progressed.

"I hope you all understand," said the lion, "that I am the villain of the play. Not because I am naturally cruel or vicious, but because it's the best part in the piece, and affords me greater opportunities to divulge my powers. I'm really very gentle and kind-hearted, and

you ought to admire me very much for appearing to be so bad. With these few words of explanation, I shall proceed, and I trust I shall not be interrupted again. Where is the lamb?"

"Here," bleated the lamb.

"Very well," said the lion; "don't paint your face too heavily, and have your hair cut."

"I can't play tragedy without long wool," complained the lamb.

"You can shave and wear a wig," decided the lion.

"Silence! silence!" echoed the monkey. "Silence in the gallery, or I'll come upstairs and crack some nuts."

All the little boys in the gallery hung breathless over the railing as the lion took the centre of the stage and declaimed·

> "In yonder glade,
>   Beneath the shade,
>   Where ne'er a spade
>   Has turned a blade,
>   A winsome maid,
>   Of lofty grade,

As tall and staid
As e'er was made,
Is but a jade,
With garments frayed,

And bills unpaid.
She'll fail and fade,
Unless arrayed.
Therefore, some knight,
A lucky wight
With coin bright,
Must win the fight.
And win he will
Who pays the bill,
And I will pay that bill
  to-day.
Oh, I, her suitor,
I hope I'll suit her, — "

The author in the upper box.

"You're gagging," said the prompter.

"Yes," said the author, from an upper box, "don't take liberties with my text."

"I shall!" roared the lion. "Give me liberty, or give me death!"

The sad, lone voice moved uneasily in his seat, and murmured in his sleep.

" That was a long speech," remarked
the King of Jumbles.

" If you don't like it," said the lion,
" you can have your money back; but
you've no right to disturb the people who
are asleep."

" Well, I'll try it a little longer," said
the King.

" Just what I'm going to do," said the
lion, as he continued :

> " A vicious bear
> In yonder lair
> Hath laid a snare
> For her so fair.
> That bear I dare
> To touch a hair —

" Here the bear should interrupt me
with a hideous growl ! "

" I did," expostulated the bear.

" I didn't hear you," said the lion.

" Very well," acquiesced the bear, " I'll
do it again : ' Er-r-r-r — ' "

" A little more emphasis, please," said
the lion.

" Er-r-r-r-r," growled the bear.

"I don't think your elocution is good," remarked the lion, "but let that pass, — where was I?"

"Just after the growl, please," replied the prompter.

"Ah, yes," said the lion, lighting a cigarette:

> "I hear his roar,
> But ere his jaw
> Can yawn once more,
> His blood shall pour
> Upon the floor —
> Upon the floor —
> Upon the floor —

"How many times," asked the lion, sitting down, "how many times am I to say 'upon the floor?' That's your cue, and you ought to spring upon me from behind that lamp-post."

"I beg your pardon," said the bear, "but I was playing penny-ante with the tom-cat; where were you?"

"Upon the floor," said the lion.

"I know," said the bear, "but where were you?"

" Upon the floor," said the lion.

" Yes, yes," said the bear, " but where — "

" It's the cue," said the prompter; " upon the floor."

" Oh," said the bear, " I see, — now I
jump." And the bear jumped.

" Don't jump in front of me," said the
lion ; " they can't see me."

" I beg your pardon," meekly replied
the bear. " I was carried away by my
part."

" Don't let it carry you in front of me
again," answered the lion.

> " What, ho ! I fear
> This villain here !
> This loathsome beast ! "

roared the bear.

" Stop ! " said the lion, " you interpolated
that last line ! "

" How's that, prompter? " appealed the
bear.

" He's gone out to luncheon," said the
call boy.

" If we can't have fair play," said the

lion, "it's no use playing,—it isn't artistic!"

"Bah!" said the bear.

"Boo!" said the lion.

"I'll have no quarrelling," said Noah.

"My hated rival" (said the lion), "I will away!
To-morrow you shall die at break of day.
The time has come when you shall cease to
    scoff;
I'll wed the maid you love, ha, ha, and off."

"'Ha, ha, and off,'" said the prompter, "is only a stage direction. You shouldn't have said it."

"It doesn't say so," said the lion.

"But you did," replied the prompter.

"I said so," said the lion, "and I can't play any more. I've just received a letter from my mother, and she's not feeling well, and she wishes me to return home; therefore, you'll have to excuse me."

"Very well," said the prompter.

"Ah, you are there," said Miss Tabby, who was dressed in a divided skirt, because she had given half of it to her sister.

"Ah, you are there, my dearest, dearest surr ;
  Ah, let me perch upon your knee and purr ;
  Ah, let me stroke your whiskers with my
      cheek ;
  Ah, let me squat upon my knees and squeak ;
  Ah, let me sigh and simper, droop my head,
  And throw myself in tears upon my bed ;
  Ah, let me coax and cozzen, kiss and tease ; —
  Or anything you please to please to please."

"I do not understand the plot," said
the King of Jumbles.

"There isn't any," said Mrs. Piggy
Wiggy; "there isn't any, and you mustn't
interrupt it, — we don't want plots. You've
received a souvenir programme, haven't
you?"

"Yes," said the King.

"Well, that's all," said Mrs. Piggy
Wiggy.

"Is it over?" asked the sad, lone voice,
waking up with a start. "Is it? Thank
goodness gracious I have done my duty
and I may depart, — I have been here and
I may go. I have seen nothing and heard
nothing, and it is over. Shut your eyes

and you will see what I see; open them and you will see nothing. Woe,—woe,— ha, ha!" And gradually, before the very eyes of Beatrice and Jessie, this strange being dissolved into tears; a tiny rivulet flowing swiftly up the centre aisle was all their astonished gaze beheld. Yet even as the stream rippled over the floor its fleeting spirit murmured, "Woe,—woe,—ha, ha!" and the very benches reëchoed on either hand, "Woe,—woe,—ha, ha!"

"It is time," said Noah, taking a birch rod out of his pocket, "to go to school."

"Everybody must stand up when I come in," said the schoolmaster. "Anybody who's brought me something may go up top; all the boys and girls who haven't brought me anything, may go down bottom."

"Please, sir," said the lean boy, "the fat boy is stealing my apples."

"Very well," said the schoolmaster, "since you have been foolish enough to lose your apples, you can't have them, and since the fat boy has acquired them dishonestly, he can't enjoy them. Lay them on my desk. It is an ill wind," moralized the schoolmaster, "that blows nobody anything. I will ask the fat boy to recite a poem, and he must stand on the form."

The fat boy wept.

"Dry your tears," said the schoolmaster; "it's only a matter of form."

The fat boy climbed on to the bench, and having withdrawn his fists from his pockets and squeezed them into his eyes, extended his mouth to its utmost and recited with much feeling the following simple lines :

> "Maid of Fashions, ere I start,
> Give, oh, give me back my tart ;
> Or, since that is in your chest,
> Keep it now, and take my vest ;
> You're my Annie, I'm your Joe, —
> Zoedone. Sapolio."

"Where is Greece?" said the schoolmaster.

"On my pinafore," said the pale girl.

"Does anybody here know anything?" inquired the schoolmaster.

"No!" replied all the boys and girls in unison.

"Very well," said the schoolmaster, "that is why I am here; that is what I am paid for. If I told you anything you'd know it, and then I'd have to leave. What's the capital of England?"

"Money," said Beatrice.

"Right!" said the schoolmaster, "but you shouldn't have said so; it's silly to give it away. Who has a clean pocket-handkerchief?"

"Nobody," said everybody.

"I'm sorry," reflected the schoolmaster, with a sigh; "I was going to beat the boy with a clean pocket-handkerchief, and I am sadly in need of exercise. The thin girl may recite while I take a nap."

The thin girl rose and rose and rose until she reached the ceiling, and recited to the harmonious accompaniment of an accordion played by the fat boy:

"O Jimmy boy, why kiss a toy,
  When Polly sits a-weeping?
And all about a Jimmy lout, —
  Be up, for time is fleeting!
If eyes are red and lips do pout,
  You ought to cure the sorrow;
Do you believe that she will
    grieve,
  My lad, for you, to-morrow?
Ah, never let a tear-drop fall
  That Jimmy does not treasure,
So foll de roll and dance with
    Poll, —
  She says she will, with pleasure."

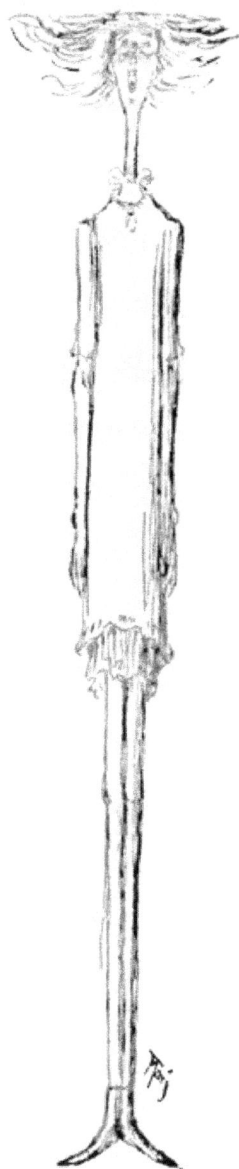

Beatrice and Jessie concluded that this was an amiable invitation to leave the schoolroom, and donning their waterproofs, as it was raining, and carefully strapping their lunch tins over their shoulders, and with still greater care hiding their schoolbooks where they would never find them again, they hastened out of the schoolhouse.

A wild burst of alarm startled the welkin as the two children realized that during their foolish absence in the Ark the water had risen mountain high all around them, and that unless some steamer or sailing vessel came without delay to their rescue, they would immediately be drowned. For days they strained their eyes until they were nearly broken, searching the scorched horizon for a vessel. There was water, water everywhere, but they didn't care to drink it. Hunger visited them, but they said they were out. Sleep refused to close their weary eyelids, and their chilled limbs turned different colors, — which was the only kaleidoscopic entertainment they enjoyed.

At last, one day Jessie turned red, white, and blue.

"A flag! a flag!" cried Beatrice. "A British ship. Sail, ho! sail, ho!" and sank back, exhausted, on the raft.

The ship hove in sight upon the offing, in the very nick of time. One moment more and all would have been over, and this stirring narrative ended. Beatrice and Jessie had opened their last box of sardines and drank their last bottle of warm milk. Nothing now remained but some jars of Boston baked beans.

Nearer and nearer approached the ship. Would she see them, and if so, how? Was there a watch on the forecastle, and, if so, was it going?

The approaching vessel suddenly sighted them, and recklessly throwing its head up into the wind, she lay rocking gently, as if at anchor, whilst the captain, who was sitting in the crow's nest, sang a lullaby.

A boat was lowered from the davits and rowed towards them, but the tension had been too great; hope had been deferred too long; with a little gasp, they fell back, inanimate, upon the floe of ice that had carried them thus far.

It was years when they awoke. It seemed but a day, — an hour. With difficulty they gathered their scattered senses. Where, — where were they? The creaking of timbers, the groans of the cordage, the green swirl of the waters against the small round port over their berth, — and the horrible truth dawned upon them; and by some mutual impulse, indefinable, but none the less irresistible, they cried, "Steward! steward!"

How long they might have remained in this situation, it is impossible to say.

They might have been there still, had not
the steamer by some curious chance arrived somewhere.

"Where are we?" said Beatrice and
Jessie to the captain.

As the captain does not concern us,
and will play no important part in this
narrative, it will perhaps be as well to
waste a few moments upon the description
of a man who cannot possibly interest us.
The captain was perhaps rather under
than over-sized, although his great breadth
of girth, combined with an unusual pro-
tuberance, imparted more the appearance
of obesity than of strength. His lower
limbs, in direct contrast to his upper spars,
were chiselled down to mere shavings,
whilst his features were so beaten and
battered by wind and storm as to be un-
recognizable. Upon his bald head, and
in order to afford it that protection which
nature had denied it, he wore a night-
cap; and one arm hung limp in its sleeve,
it having been lost in a battle with the
Turks, and to the elbow was attached an

iron hook, with which the captain could read, write, and arithmetic. By common consent, any reference on board ship to the painful occasion upon which the captain's arm took its hook was avoided. Such was the captain of the *Corsair*, a ninety-nine hundred gun frigate of the fifth form or class.

But we have wandered from our tale. When Beatrice and Jessie asked the captain where they were, he opened his mouth and shivered.

"Are you cold?" asked Beatrice.

"Silly," said the captain, "did you never hear that I am compelled to shiver my timbers before I can answer any question? But let that pass." The captain rolled a quid of tobacco in his mouth, and cast his eye to windward.

Beatrice and Jessie expostulated, but the deed was done.

"We are," said the captain, "on the Spanish main, where rich treasure-ships are far more plentiful than apples or oranges."

At this moment, the lookout reported a strange sail to leeward.

" The fact that we are raising that ship. hand over hand, and that we sail two feet to her one, proves conclusively that we are the faster of the two."

It was with such reasonings as these that the captain maintained the discipline of his crew, and retained the respect, — nay, the reverence of his men.

" Look out below," cried the captain.

" Aye, aye, sir," answered the cabin boy.

" How many bells is it ? "

" Ten, sir," said the cabin boy.

" Deduct two," said the captain, " and pipe all hands to dinner."

" Deduct one more," said the first luff, "and we'll take a drink."

The captain, who was a person of an amiable disposition, assented; the boat-swain struck seven bells, and all hands having gone below, soon no sound, other than the agreeable gurgle of liquids in transmission, disturbed the soporific still-ness of the summer air.

"Have you ever been engaged?" said the powder-monkey to Beatrice.

"Never," answered Beatrice, indignantly. (Five of her blown-away sisters had been engaged to the same boy, and the question awakened painful memories.)

"Well, then, you're likely to be," said the powder-monkey. "That Spanish Don is an enemy of mine, and we're going to have a battle."

"I don't see how that concerns me," answered Beatrice.

"Oh, don't you?" said the powder-monkey. "You'll see pretty soon, when yonder Don runs athwart your hawse, and fires a broadside into your bread-locker."

No doubt the powder-monkey would have continued in this strain for some time, had not the admiral of the fleet signalled to the *Corsair* for the powder-monkey to go below and stop talking, as the admiral wished to have a nap previous to inditing a poem before the battle.

The powder-monkey stole carefully forward, and having stealthily raised his nose above the rim of the bulwark, he lifted the thumb of his right hand with great precision to that feature, and signalled the admiral his passive and polite acquiescence. He then threw off his coat, kicked off his boots, and dived below. This manœuvre was not executed a moment too soon, for barely had he disappeared before a round shot, whistling through the rigging, took off the very place where his head would have been. A jeering laugh resounded from the hold.

The deck steward brought Beatrice and Jessie a couple of deck chairs and two basins of beef tea. Also, two agreeable young men wrapped their little feet up in nice warm rugs.

" Is there any danger? " asked Jessie.

" None whatever," replied the surgeon, " and if there were, you shouldn't mind it, when I am here ; " whereupon the surgeon placed on the deck a pot of hot glue, a bottle of mucilage, a chisel, some nails, a hammer, and four packages of court-plaster.

Beatrice shuddered at the sight of these ominous and telltale preparations, and would no doubt have sought refuge in her cabin, had not rapidly succeeding events pursued each other so swiftly as to draw her attention in another direction, and thereby divert her thoughts elsewhere.

Whilst these circumstances had transpired, the ships had rapidly neared each other; the port-holes had been thrown wide open, and the guns cleared for action. The decks, also, had been greased with vaseline, in order to make the movement of the belligerent crews as rapid as possible.

The donkey in the donkey engine, utilized to turn the great swivel gun, had gotten up all steam, and was braying vigorously, whilst the Highlanders on their bagpipes with strident note were calling the horse-marines to their stations. All was pandemonium and excitement. Everything presaged a long and bloodthirsty conflict. A crisp breeze was blowing

and whitening the crests of the waves,
whilst the dark blue of the ocean, re-
flecting as it did the azure of the sky,
composed a stirring picture of nature's
moving energy and man's ceaseless enterprise, — together with the music of the
bagpipes and the incessant braying of
the ass.

At this instant, one gun fired by the
British flag-ship called all hands to attention, and a large white flag or tablecloth
was descried to unfurl itself at her main
royal masthead.   At the same time, the
Admiral himself, attired in full evening
dress, was seen to be standing on the
poop or quarter-deck upon a raised plat-
form, consisting of two barrels crossed by
a plank.

The agility with which this celebrated
naval commander balanced himself, with
the assistance of a pole, upon this frail
bridge, had gained for him a world-wide
renown.   And now as the two navies,
drawn up as they were in battle array,
beheld this famed warrior in the very

performance of the dauntless feat which had won for him the esteem of every sailor in the world, not only the navy which he led, but the entire complement of the opposing fleet, resounded with an ecstacy of prolonged cheering.

But this exhibition of prowess was to be succeeded by an even more comprehensive display of nautical efficiency. Again the gun boomed, and it was perceived that the British Admiral was holding in one hand a document, whilst the other contained, in place of the balancing pole, a long speaking-trumpet, with which, whilst he failed not to preserve his equilibrium, he delivered the following moving hymn before the battle:

" I am monarch of all I survey, —
    My attitude none can dispute !
Tho' my centre of gravity may,
    It cannot upset my repute.

" By this petrified pose which I boast
    That no nation can rob of its calm,
Tho' the sea may be storming its most,
    I'm impervious to any alarm !

" 'Tis this wonderful stoical face
    That never betrays an emotion,
This marvellous, inanimate grace,
    That crowns me the King of the Ocean !

" I'm out of humanity's reach, —
    It may canter or gallop or waddle ;
I've not as much vim as a leech,
    And my face is as void as my noddle.

" I'm an Englishman, proud of my race ;
    I boast of my lack of emotion, —
It's this wonderful, stoical face
    That crowns me the King of the Ocean !

" You may fire your guns if you will,
    You may pelt with torpedoes and shot,
My nose remains perfectly still,
    It is not to be stirred from the spot.

" 'Tis true I may wax somewhat pale,
    Yet I'll vow by my British repose,
Tho' my centre of gravity fail,
    No! you cannot disturb my old nose.

" I'm an Englishman, proud of my race ;
    I'm proud of my lack of emotion, —
It's my wonderful stoical face
    That crowns me the King of the Ocean ! "

Barely had these thrilling words been uttered, than the boys on the Spanish Armada, swarming up the yards, opened a well-directed fire on the Admiral with their pea-shooters. Although the shot fell like hail about him, and the noise made by the pellets striking his chest was not unlike the sound of rain upon a tin roof, the Admiral retained his immovable and dignified posture. The only notice indeed that he vouchsafed the storm of bullets was to open his umbrella and sit down on the deck beneath its cool and protecting shade.

It is impossible to describe the anguish which Beatrice and Jessie now suffered.

The entire Spanish Armada had advanced to the attack. The air was thick with missiles of every description. Bricks, boots, and invectives volleyed and thundered. Beatrice and Jessie choking down the screams which rose involuntarily to their lips, hastily tied red crosses on their arms, and tenderly nursed the wounded.

The Spanish Admiral had formed his fleet into a corkscrew, and was trying to draw the English ships. Again and again he exerted all his strength. In vain. The British stuck to their bottles.

It was now evident that if anything was to be accomplished, something must be done. Hoisting a flag of truce, the Spanish withdrew for a consultation.

The English were permitted to catch their breath. But their exertions had been so tremendous that they sank to a man upon the decks of their vessels, and stared with meaningless and bloodshot eyes before them, whilst their lips mumbled rambling and senseless words.

Beatrice and Jessie carried water to the

poor sailors, and tried to persuade them
to drink it, but failed. A dense fog caused
by the discussion in the air now envel-
oped the combatants in its grateful folds,
and obscured them from each other, an
event which was taken full advantage of
by both fleets; for when the mist rolled
away and the moon illuminated the scene,
neither fleet was in sight.

It was with deep regret that Beatrice
and Jessie parted from the many friends
they had acquired during their passage,
and they cordially invited the captain to
come and see them as soon as they knew
where they were to live.

After landing, Beatrice and Jessie wandered towards a beautiful park, the gates
of which stood invitingly open. Their
little dog gamboled merrily before them,
and its joyous barks and wagging tail
expressed louder than words the happiness he anticipated.

" Leave the dog outside," said the policeman.

" He *is* outside," answered Beatrice and

Jessie, "we didn't like to leave the poor
dear little love at home."

"He can't go into the park," said the
policeman.

"Why?" asked Beatrice and Jessie.

"He'd eat the grass," replied the policeman. "Leave him with me, and I'll give
you a check."

"For how much?" asked Jessie.

"For the dog," said the policeman.

The children had to leave their pet
in the care of the policeman, who gave
them a brass check with a number on
it, and they walked into the park. Being
fatigued they sat down on the grass under
a tree.

"Get up!" said the policeman.

"Why?" said Beatrice and Jessie.

"You're spoiling the grass."

"Can't we sit on the grass?"

"No," said the policeman.

Beatrice and Jessie were walking away,
when the policeman stopped them.

"You can't walk over the grass," he
said.

"'I'M DIFFERENT,' SAID THE POLICEMAN."

" How are we to reach the path ? " they asked.

" I'll carry you," said the policeman. " If you walked over the grass it would never grow again."

" But *you* are walking on it," they exclaimed.

" I'm different," said the policeman ; and tucking them under his arms, he carried them to the nearest gravel path.

" This is very tiresome," said Beatrice. " I think I'll pick some flowers and make a wreath."

" If you pick any flowers," said the policeman. " I'll have to lock you up."

Beatrice and Jessie began to cry.

" Don't cry in the park," said the policeman. " If you want to cry, you must go outside."

" Then I'll ride on a bicycle," said Beatrice. "I must do something."

" Very well," said the policeman.

Beatrice and Jessie mounted two bicycles, and were just about to start off when a large cart dumped a hill of gravel right in front of them and they fell off their wheels. Beatrice and Jessie were so disgusted that they stood quite still in the middle of the path with their thumbs in their mouths.

" Move on !" said the policeman. " You mustn't stand still in the park."

" Oh, dear! oh, dear!" said Beatrice, " what can we do ? "

" Why don't you fly ? " said the robin.

" We can't," answered Beatrice.

" Oh, yes, you can," replied the robin. " You only think you can't because you've never tried. What you lack is confidence. If you believe you can fly, you can fly. You ought to be ashamed of yourselves! Great girls like you to be outdone by a little robin ! Why, even flies fly ! "

" You mustn't fly in the park !" said the policeman.

But Beatrice and Jessie, fired by the example set them by the worthy robin, and no doubt excited by the tyranny of the policeman, rose in the air and flew out of sight.

"They're flying-machines," said the policeman, as he sat down to whittle a stick. "I'm sorry I spoke to them, I thought they were girls."

All the birds were extremely polite to Beatrice and Jessie, and they soon discovered that they had acted wisely in entrusting themselves to the care of the robin, who seemed to stand very high in the estimation of his brother birds.

"If you don't mind," said the robin, "the rooks are giving a big party this afternoon, and we will go there."

"With pleasure," said Beatrice and Jessie.

When they arrived at the Rookery, they found the mansion crowded to suffocation.

"Dear! dear!" said the robin, as he squeezed his way through the door, followed by the girls, "this is certainly a crush."

"Where's the hostess?" asked Beatrice.

"Oh, that doesn't matter," said the robin, "she's somewhere, perhaps on the roof. You'll have to climb the stairs if you want to speak to her. But first we'd better fight for something to eat."

Beatrice and Jessie were fighting girls and assented gladly. Robin layed vigorously about him with fists and beak, while Beatrice and Jessie kicked and scratched and bit until they reached a long table behind which a number of birds in black and white liveries were dealing out food and drink just as fast as they could; and the children noticed that the perspiration was streaming from their faces.

" Grab all you can," said the robin.

Beatrice snatched a handful of ice-cream, whilst Jessie packed her apron with apricot jelly.

" Come along," said the robin, who had tucked his pockets full of everything he could lay his hands on. " Come along, and we'll eat it." But alas! there is many a slip. Some late arrivals attacked them with so much vehemence that in a little while they had been robbed of all their hard won refreshments.

"It's no good crying over spilt milk," said the robin. "Pin yourselves together again and I'll present you to Mrs. Rook."

After a struggle through the crowd they found Mrs. Rook at the head of the staircase; she had one arm in a sling and the other was fast becoming useless. But she shook hands with Beatrice and Jessie, and hoped they were enjoying themselves. Behind the hostess a little cock sparrow was playing on the piano, and further away a small parrot was talking as fast as he could for the amusement of the crowd. A tall blackbird was also reciting a poem.

"That's our great tragedian," said the robin. "I know him, and if you like I'll ask him to recite something for us."

"I don't like to trouble him," said Beatrice.

"Oh, he likes it," said the robin; "he recites all the time, and he'd be very unhappy if we didn't ask him. Moreover, he'll have to recite for me, or I'd write things about him in my newspaper."

" Do you write newspapers ? " asked Jessie.

" Yes," said the robin ; " I write news-papers and poetry and things. If you like, I'll make the blackbird recite my latest poem."

" Oh, do ! " said Beatrice.

When the blackbird saw the robin, he wept for joy, and the robin himself was so deeply affected that he mingled his tears with those of the blackbird.

" Recite my poem," said the robin. The blackbird wept again. " My latest," added the robin.

" I know it ; I know it well," said the blackbird, and wept. " It is a touching poem, a beautiful and moving song."

The robin flew swiftly among the crowd, and hastily imparted the information that the great blackbird was about to declaim his poem. Instantly all was attention, and every one talked as loud as he could. The blackbird, advancing one leg and throwing back the hair from his low brow, announced "The Cuckoo Song, by my lifelong friend, Mr. Robin : "

"The cuckoo does not earn his food ;
　He's not industrious or good, —
　He waits till others build a cot,
　And then he steals the house and lot ;
　He does not make the beds or sweep ;
　He does not go to mart, or keep
　The little children clean for school,
　Or scrub the floor or card the wool ;
　He does not boil or fry or stew, —
　Oh, no, — he simply sings 'Cuckoo.'
　But robins build their nests, and say :
　'We have no time to play to-day.' "

Mr. Blackbird paused. Taking off his eye-glasses, and changing his voice to a deep and hollow tone, he continued :

"The cuckoo goes to ball and rout ;
　He's never in ; he's always out ;
　And while he lives on cake and ale,
　His little brothers pine and pale.
　He plays at every club in town,
　But will not buy his wife a gown !

> At parties he is full of grace,
> And when at home he pulls a face, —
> You'd think that he would smile there too?
> Oh, no! he simply sings 'Cuckoo.'
> But robins build their nests, and say:
> 'We have no time to play to-day.'"

Mr. Blackbird replaced his glasses, and permitted a playful smile to curl about his lips, as he looked keenly about him:

> "The cuckoo is a thievish bird,
> As you have very often heard.
> At afternoons, when weather's damp,
> He always takes the newest gamp;
> He also steals your latest tale,
> For which he ought to go to jail.
> He does not wait on Ma and Jane,
> And hand the salads and champagne, —
> Oh, no! But I have seen him sneak
> Enough cigars to last a week;
> And will he leave some smokes for you?
> Oh, no! he simply sings 'Cuckoo.'
> But robins build their nests, and say:
> 'We have no time to play to-day.'"

Then, lapsing into a sentimental, nay, somewhat mournful strain, the blackbird fell gracefully into a chair, and, reclining his head upon his hand, concluded:

"The cuckoo tells the widow lies,
And wins her simple sympathies,
And chooses all your busy hours
To sing her songs or bring her flowers;
And when you reach her house for tea,
You find you've lost her property.
But will the cuckoo seize her home,
And everything you thought your own?
No, — that he will not dare to do!
Oh, yes, — he simply sings 'Cuckoo.'
But robins build their nests and say:
'We have no time to play to-day.'"

"My dear, dear children!" exclaimed some one close to Beatrice and Jessie, "Don't you know me? Have I found you at last? Embrace me. I'm your ant!"

Beatrice and Jessie turned round, and were immediately clasped in the arms of their long lost ant.

"You must come and live with me," said the ant, and was so pressing in her invitation that the children had not the heart to refuse. "It's very fortunate for you," said their ant, "that I found you. If you are going into society, I can be of immeasurable service to you. I go everywhere, — everywhere. Come along. Things are all in a heap at home, but you won't mind that."

"We didn't know we had ants," interjected Beatrice.

"Bless the child," said her ant, looking at her fondly.

"Do you really go everywhere?" asked Jessie. "Perhaps you can tell us where the prince lives who is enslaved by the boarding-house fairy?"

"Well, you see," replied the ant, scratching her nose reflectively, "there are so many boarding-houses, and we frequent them all."

Beatrice and Jessie seemed very disappointed.

"There, there," soothed the ant, "don't cry; where there's a will, there's a way, —

that's the ant motto,—— and I shouldn't wonder if some member or other of our family
would be able to direct you."

On the road to the ant's residence, they
met a great many of their relatives, who
appeared to be too occupied to take any
notice of them.

" They're very rude," said the ant. " If
there is anything in the world worth living for, it's etiquette."

" It's what ? " asked Beatrice and Jessie.

" Etiquette ! " shouted the ant, bridling
and looking severe. " What would society
be, if people didn't bow to one another,
and dress well, and be particular about
their finger-nails and their hats and bon-
nets ?   I shudder," continued the ant,
' whenever I see a badly dressed woman
in church.   It's terrible to think of what
might happen to her ! Of all places where
a woman should be got up in the very
height of fashion, it's church."

" I don't think your grammar is good,
ant," said Jessie, who was precocious.

" That doesn't matter," said the ant;

"I'm well dressed. Moreover," continued the ant, reflectively, as she courteously returned the bow of an elderly and gentlemanly ant in a Prince Albert and a high silk hat, "moreover, I have money, and my coachman is immaculate, though I say it as shouldn't. I can do without grammar. You can't eat grammar, can you?" she inquired. "You can't buy gowns with it, or horses and carriages, or diamonds, or a French cook, or steam yachts, or boxes at the opera, or castles and parks in England, can you?"

When the ant had ceased speaking, she said no more. A cloud was seen approaching. It was a cloud of dust. The dust was sand. This cloud of sand was a simoon. A simoon is the dreaded sand-storm of the desert. What was a simoon doing in London? We shall see. It approached with frightful rapidity. The inhabitants fled before it. Some hid in the cellars; others retired to their beds, and drew the covering over their heads. Beatrice and Jessie were much alarmed. The ant exhibited no concern; she remarked:

"Sand is my native element. Sand is breath to my nostrils." The ant then walked home.

It is impossible to exaggerate the peril of the children's situation. If their lives were to be saved, some refuge must swiftly be found. Where was this refuge? Was it at hand? Unbeknown to them, it was. This refuge was a four-wheeler. The person who drove this four-wheeler was a man. This cannot be said of all persons who control the destinies of a four-wheeler. What is a four-wheeler? A four-wheeler is a common or garden cab. It has four wheels. It has also shafts. In the shafts is an animal. Is this animal a horse? Who can tell?

Beatrice hailed the cab. The cab stopped. Why did the cab stop? The driver had spoken to the horse. What had he said? He had said, "Whoa." Was the driver a North American Indian? He was not. He was an Irishman. An Irishman is a man who does not live in Ireland. What is Ireland? It is an island. What are its principal products? Pigs, potatoes, and politics.

Beatrice and Jessie were about to entrust their fortunes to this honest Irishman. The Irishman's hand was extended. Beatrice and Jessie paused. This pause was fatal to the Irishman. It is in a moment that fortunes are lost,— this moment proved such an one. The sky had cleared, the sand-storm had passed.

The cab was dismissed and the Arab rode away calling his prophet names. The sun now shone with undiminished splendor upon the plain. The heat was terrific. The very trees and rocks were broiling. There was a smell of cooking in the air. The flowers hung their heads in listless apathy.

The children were exhausted,— their feet refused to carry them further. They sat down. Some cocoanuts falling upon their bare heads attracted their attention.

" These nuts," said Beatrice, " contain

an agreeable liquid which closely resembles milk. The fruit of the nut itself, although indigestible, is not unpalatable."

Robinson Crusoe was out for the day, visiting his plantations and removing sacks of flour and jewelry from the wreck. He had nailed a card to the door of his office which read, "Will return at 5 P. M." The children exercised the liberty of using his gimlet and his axe to obtain refreshment from the cocoanut. They intended to remain some few days with Mr. Robinson Crusoe and his man Friday. Whilst awaiting their return, the parrot entertained them with songs and humorous anecdotes. The children marvelled greatly at the intelligence of this remarkable bird.

" Perhaps," said Beatrice, when the parrot had concluded a song and dance even more entertaining than its fellows, " since you have displayed so much wisdom, you can impart some information concerning the prince who is enslaved by the boarding-house fairy ? "

" Young ladies," replied the parrot, " I have always been too much interested in the fortunes of Haroun Alraschid, to forget any circumstance of the incidents of his life which has been handed down to us.   If you choose to honor me with your attention, I shall immediately gratify your curiosity."

Beatrice and Jessie testified their wish to hear the relation, and the parrot, who was no other than the Sultana Scheherazade, began in these words :

" Before relating the adventures of the renowned Commander of the Faithful, which would occupy a period of three years, permit me to state that the prince of whom you are in search is no other than the Caliph Haroun Alraschid himself, and that the fairy who has enslaved the pride of the Moslem race is the same wicked Genie who, tired of hearing my stories in praise of the great monarch, transformed me into a parrot. Giafar, the Grand Vizier to the Caliph, and who shared with him his nocturnal adventures, is allowed to remain in companionship with his master. Should you find the prince, you would also discover his devoted servant, Giafar. I have no doubt whatever that if you succeed in releasing the Caliph from the spell of the Genie you will earn his lifelong gratitude, and that he will load you with wealth and honors. When this occurs, do not forget the unfortunate Scheherazade." The parrot was silent; but the tears that flowed down her beak testified more than words to the anguish of her soul.

"Believe us," said Beatrice, "we will try to remember your name."

"I will give you my card and address," said the parrot, "and I will now offer you such advice as may be acceptable in your situation. Follow your nose for five leagues; it will lead you within the vicinity of the boarding-house. When you have arrived you will be apprised of the fact by the odor, which is unmistakable. Here you will discover a youth searching the contents of an ash-barrel. This youth will be no other than the unfortunate Giafar. He will lead you into the presence of the Commander of the Faithful. More I am not at liberty to disclose. Haroun Alraschid will furnish you with further particulars."

Although the children used every means to persuade the parrot to continue, she was silent, and beyond saying at intervals, "Pretty Poll, lump of sugar," her mouth was sealed.

Robinson Crusoe had now returned. On his way to his hut he had discovered a hansom cab and horse which had been blown ashore in the gale of the previous night. In the cab he had found a parcel containing a dozen six-button gloves, size five and a half, but notwithstanding he had carefully searched the beach in every direction, he had discovered no clue to the young and beautiful owner. He had climbed upon the cab and had driven himself to his hut. Friday was now un-harnessing the horse and stabling it in the shed with the tame ostrich, the providential pig, and the miraculous cow.

Robinson Crusoe, when he entered his drawing - room, where the two young ladies were seated, was attired in the very height of fashion. In-deed, with a man of Robinson Crusoe's refined taste, it could not be otherwise, since his island provided everything.

Beatrice and Jessie rose respectfully when Robinson Crusoe entered, but he begged them to be seated and to enjoy some of the delicacies which Friday would place before them.

Friday, attired in the Crusoe livery, entered and deposited on a table some

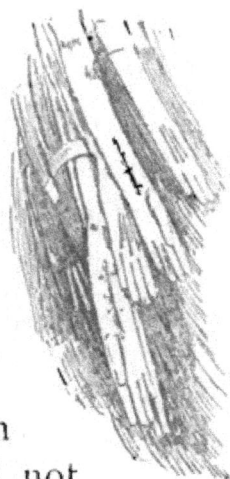

excellent ortolans (fried and served with risotto), a most tempting paté de foie gras, several large bunches of hothouse grapes, some exquisite cakes and a decanter of dry Tokay.

" Most heartily," said Robinson Crusoe, rising and bowing with much grace, " I bid you welcome to my house, which, together with its owner, is entirely at your disposal. I beg you will partake of this poor refreshment until a repast more worthy of the honor you have done me may be prepared. And in the meanwhile my faithful retainer and myself will accomplish our best to lighten the hours of waiting."

Robinson Crusoe and Friday now withdrew, but presently returned in the costume affected by the clowns at a country fair. Lightly leaping over one another after the manner adopted in the popular game of leap-frog, they circled about the room, exchanging hearty slaps or such witticisms as were not beyond the comprehension of the young and unsophisticated. This was followed by a most dexterous ventriloquial entertainment on the part of Robinson Crusoe, his man Friday having been stationed on the roof in order to reply down the chimney to the questions propounded to him by his master. After this, a sleight-of-hand performance by Friday enabled Robinson Crusoe to withdraw for a period. Friday's tricks were truly astonishing, and consisted in making an omelette in Beatrice's hat, and in causing anything in the shape of money or valuables to disappear. When this fund of humor had been exhausted, Robinson Crusoe returned with a violin, and having carefully tuned it with the assistance of a grand piano, which he had found firmly wedged in a cleft of rock some few weeks ago, he accompanied Friday to the following characteristic song:

" Dar's noding on dis island dat yer can't get
    free !
      Boom de boom de rido !
From a green omberella to a mango-tree,
      Boom de boom de rido !

Dar's a roasted possum down der chimney
  flue,
And he's stuffed wid onion and wid chest-
  nuts, too!
De milk and honey is flowing down de street;
It's a slap-up island, and it can't be beat
  No how! Boom de boom de rido!"

Here Robinson Crusoe and Friday
paused in their melody to execute a lively
and exhilarating dance; they then continued:

"Dar's noding on dis island dat yer have der
  do,
    Boom de boom de rido!
Yer just sit still and it walks ter you,
    Boom de boom de rido!
Dar ain't no troubles, and dar ain't no crime,
But it's balm o' Gilead all der time.
And dar ain't no taxes, and dar ain't no care,
But it's summer and sunshine all der year,
    You bet! Boom de boom de rido!"

Robinson Crusoe and his man again
performed a rapid shuffle and proceeded:

" Dar's noding on dis island dat dar ain't
    thrown in,
       Boom de boom de rido !
When yer buys de oxen, why yer buys der
    skin,
       Boom de boom de rido !
If you buys a melon, why you buy de patch ;
If yer buys a chicken, why she's bound to
    hatch ;
If yer kiss and yer caught and marries yer
    Sall,
Why all har relations dey goes wid der gal.
    Just so, hey ! Boom de boom de rido ! "

Beatrice and Jessie stole on tiptoe from
the room. As long as the fate of the
prince remained in doubt, they could not
enter into the spirit of this gay and frolic-
some scene. Scarcely had they proceeded
fifteen miles before they discovered a re-
cumbent figure in an attitude of great
dejection beneath an olive-tree.

" Stranger," said Beatrice, striking the
youth violently on the back with the palm
of her hand, and addressing him with
great diffidence, " your attitude interests

me. Tell me what has caused you to cast yourself in such evident sorrow beneath this tree ? "

" O light of my eyes," replied the youth, screening his face with his hands, and gazing at Beatrice and Jessie between the outspread fingers, " know that I am the unhappy Boubou; but alas! my name will convey no meaning to your ears. Suffice it that I am the son of a millionaire who reared me in the expectation of securing my living without having to work for it. Alas, how were my hopes shattered! Scarcely had I reached the age of thirty-two when my stern parent called me before him. ' O Boubou,' said he, ' the time is now arrived when you must prove yourself worthy of the tender care I have bestowed upon your education.' I threw myself at his feet, but he hastily moved them under the table. ' O my father,' I replied, ' command me. Am I not your son ? ' For some time my father did not reply, but was lost in deep thought.

"'Boubou,' he then continued, 'I have determined you shall wed the lovely Moumou; her dowry is twenty million gold pieces, and I will bestow upon you a like sum.' This decision on the part of my father overwhelmed me with joy, for I had often surreptitiously watched the lovely Moumou in the garden of her mother's house, which adjoined my father's property. I did not, however, permit my father to discover the full extent of my satisfaction, but merely signified my willingness to obey him in all things. Not to weary you, O lady, with details that cannot interest you, we were married, and lived happily upon our modest competence, until one day Moumou introduced the game of croquet into our quiet home. Since that hour we have known neither peace nor happiness." The stranger ceased, but Beatrice and Jessie beheld his abstracted gaze riveted in terror upon a woman who approached, holding in her hand a croquet mallet. Scrambling to his feet, the wretched Boubou bounded away like a gazelle, pursued by the infatuated Moumou.

The children proceeded on their path, pondering on the mutability of human affairs.

The sun, golden in the morning, now changed its hue to red, and, setting in the west, bathed all the landscape in its rosy dye. Beatrice and Jessie floated on radiant clouds of scarlet ether, which, propelled by gentle zephyrs, wafted them to the north. Giant palms swayed in the cooler breeze, and myriad gaudy butterflies and jewelled humming-birds swarmed about them. Below in the valley, where the mists obscured the certainty of view, the gray willows fringed a twining stream that shone weird and white as the moon sailed majestically into its nightly empire.

The children shuddered and drew together. The clouds that bore them had turned to silver gauze and chilled their feet. The Erl-King spoke to them and waved to his daughters, who, partly shrouded in the high grasses and the wreaths of fog, danced by the brook below. The tree-toad admonished them ever and ever: "Go on! Go on! Go on!" The fickle will-o'-the-wisp beckoned them to the marshes, and an orchestra of crickets played a fantasia that thrilled the night. Some fatal spell held them in its power. Suddenly the clang of a bell, the vibrations of a gong, burst upon their ears. The landscape faded, the Erl-King and his daughters fled. The will-o'-the-wisp disappeared, — the tree-toad was silent. The crickets' orchestra died away. The flowers fell and changed to ashes. The butterflies and humming-birds flew in one dense swarm to the horizon. A pungent odor assailed their nostrils.

" Hash!" said Jessie.

" Hash!" said Beatrice.

" Look!" cried Jessie. And they looked. They found they were in a long, narrow, and squalid street. A gas-lamp burned dimly at the nearest corner. Close by, a Roman was endeavoring to grind melody

out of a box. A host of unwashed children with dishevelled hair and dingy garments danced in the noisome atmosphere.
A man slept in the gloaming of a battered
porch. The sound of a quarrelling voice
nearly drowned the asthmatic wheezing
of the organ. A black water ran in the
gutter. In this two urchins dabbled their
feet. An Oriental, bearing upon his arm
a pile of rags, cried, " Ole clos'! " Ever
and anon a lukewarm wind flapped the
yellow linen depending from a rope, and
startled the pigeons that watched them
from the roofs. A costermonger cried
his wares. A policeman twirling his club
walked boldly through the street. The
organ struck up, " Know'st thou the land
where the citron blooms ? "

" Why do people live here ? " asked
Beatrice.

" Why ? " said Jessie.

" The world is very large," said Beatrice.

" Very," said Jessie.

" Why don't they walk away ? " said
Beatrice.

" Why ? " said Jessie.

" Do you wish to live here? " asked a fat voice.

The children turned in its direction and beheld a stout woman holding her naked arms akimbo. Upon her head she wore a tinsel crown decorated with draggled artificial flowers. In one hand she clutched a wooden sceptre from which the gilt tracery was partly worn away. " Do you wish to live here? " repeated the stout woman.

The children were about to say " No! " when they noticed a thin, pale youth engaged in ransacking the contents of an ash-barrel.

" It is Giafar, the companion of the prince! " they exclaimed.

" Who speaks my unhappy name? " asked the youth.

" Oh, tell us, tell us," cried the children, " where is the prince."

" Follow me," said Giafar, " and I will lead you to him."

Beatrice and Jessie thanked the Grand

Vizier, who, opening a heavy door, led them into a dark hall that reeked of cheap cookery.

"Walk in here, young ladies," said Giafar, "and I will advise the prince of your presence. Permit me, however, to make a light."

Giafar, with some lingering remnant of a departed grace, struck a match upon the seat of his nether garment and lighted the gas; then bowing, he left the room.

"Do you wish to live here?" asked the stout woman, standing in the door.

"Who are you?" asked Beatrice.

"I am the boarding-house fairy," replied the stout lady, "and because of your extreme youth, I overlook your evident lack of courtesy. You have not answered my question. Do you wish to live here?"

"We came to find the prince," said Beatrice.

"Yes," said the boarding-house fairy, "so does every one who lives in my house.

They all want to find the prince. If it were not for him, I should be without boarders. My house would be empty. Are you going to stay here?"

" We want to find the prince," answered Beatrice.

" Then you *do* wish to live here," said the fairy. " I will prepare a room for you," and with this the fairy vanished.

Beatrice and Jessie took advantage of the opportunity to look about them. The furniture was covered with black horsehair, which, gaping here and there, exposed its secrets. A table stood in the centre of the room upon a meagre rag carpet. This carpet, which was very dark, exhaled an odor of grease. The cloth hiding the table had long since abandoned any definite color. An upright piano of doubtful origin, with stained keys, filled

the space between the fireplace and the
window, and tattered music and blotted
sheets littered its surface. Upon the
table lay some time-worn novels, an ink-
pot, and many pages of foolscap closely
covered with scribbling. A stand with
birds, from which
the plumage had
been plucked, oc-
cupied a corner. A
pair of coarse lace
curtains hung be-
fore the dim win-
dows. These curtains had
been white ;   they were
now yellow, and torn in places.
They had formerly been fastened back
with blue ribbons. A soiled one remained
to testify mournfully to this fact.

In the fireplace, a paper screen, once
bright and festive, held in its sooty mesh
the remnant of a scarlet poppy. On the
mantel-shelf, a shepherd and shepherdess
under glass covers smiled eternally. The
first played on a shattered lute ; the other

held above her head a broken arm. They were separated by a black clock, upon which a dog reclined and watched the shepherdess. The tick-tick of the clock had long since ceased. There were many ticks in this house. This was the only one that stood still.

The hour was late. Beatrice and Jessie had walked far. The atmosphere was heavy. In the horsehair chairs they sank back and closed their eyes. The clock on the mantel struck the hour and played a tune whilst the dog beat time, tick-tick-tick, with his tail. The shepherd smiled his stereotyped smile at the shepherdess; she waved her broken arm above her head, and they sang:

"We stand in a state of ecstatic delight
That is properly bound by restraint,
And who would not envy a skin that's so
white,
Or a blush that is born of such paint?

"And though we are closed in a prison like
this,
And dwell in a house made of glass,

We never complain that we weary of bliss,
  Or wear with the years as they pass.

" And note, we are dancing with perfect repose,
  And strum on a lute without noise,
Nor can you complain that we sing thro' the
    nose,
  Or charge you too high for these joys !

" You mortals may droop in the worry and
    strife,
  And sicken and languish and waste,
But we remain ever the picture of life
  Embodied in pigment and paste.

" How often is love that is known by the way
  In which its sweet symptoms are shown,
Enduring as this, that is fashioned to stay,
  On the model of Darby and Joan ?

" Or can all the riot that storms in your breast
  Be compared with contentment like ours,
Where jealousy never can prey on its rest,
  Or satiety grow with the hours?

" But ere we return to the calm that ne'er pains
  And the death that is never a curse,
Implore of the fanciful poet with brains
  Not to bring us to life in his verse!"

Beatrice and Jessie awoke. They looked steadfastly at the china figures. But they were silent, and the clock ticked no more; neither did the dog wag his tail.

"Strange!" remarked Beatrice.

"Very," said Jessie. "Since the hour approaches that we are at last to see the prince, let us carefully remember the instructions impressed upon us by the rat:

"We must enter the house,
Eluding the fairy,
And discover the prince
Alone in the dairy!"

"But where is the dairy?"

"The pump is in the scullery," said the boarding-house fairy, who appeared at this moment with her sleeves turned up and wiping the perspiration from her brow with her apron. "But do you fancy you can elude me? Never, never!"

"We must resort to stratagem," said Beatrice.

"What stratagem, ha?" asked the fairy.

" Let me think," said Beatrice.

" You may, if you can," answered the fairy.

"Oh!" cried Beatrice, "look at those handsomely attired ladies and gentlemen ringing the bell of the boarding-house opposite." No sooner had Beatrice thus slyly spoken than the boarding-house fairy darted from the room and rushed out of the house.

The children grasped one another by the hand and fled in the direction in which they hoped to discover the dairy and the prince. Nor was their enterprise unrewarded. At the end of the corridor a light streaming through a half-closed door attracted their attention. They pushed it open and stood in the presence of the prince. How can words describe what they beheld ? Or how can language picture their awe, their wonder, and their joy ?

Seated in the centre of an indescribable circle, upon a mysterious throne, sat a radiant figure, so resplendent yet so nebu-

lous as to be transparent. The face of
the prince hovered in a scintillating glory
of prismatic hues that flashed and quiv-
ered and dazzled the sight. The witching
smile that played upon his lovely countenance was so alluring as to cast them
abject on their knees. The white hand
that beckoned them was gorgeous with
the pale and varying sheen of priceless
opals; yet as they sought to seize it, the
hand faded before their eyes only to
appear again where it had vanished.

Curls of gold waved about the prince's
head in coils like jewelled serpents, and
eyes of sapphire blue sought theirs with a
yearning gaze of such profound love and
longing that they burst into an eloquence
of uncontrollable sobs.

Now Beatrice remembered the words of
the rat :

"You must kiss both his eyes,
His lips and his ears,
And sit down by his side
And call for two beers."

How could she ever do that? How

could she ever master the courage to embrace that ethereal and majestic being?

"She who hesitates is lost!" said the
rat, peeping out of a hole.

Beatrice and Jessie sprang at the throne
and threw their arms about the prince.
He melted from their
grasp, and Beatrice
and Jessie hugged
themselves.

"Now sit down by
his side," said the rat.

"But where is
he?" they ex-
claimed.

Even as they spoke
they beheld the prince restored to the
spot where they had fancied him to be,
and they humbly seated themselves at
his feet.

"Call for two beers," cried the rat.

Beatrice and Jessie shouted together,
"Zwei lager!"

Hardly had the words passed their lips
when the house was shaken by a frightful

clap of thunder, piercing shrieks resounded on every side, the doors and windows burst open, and a motley throng, with dishevelled locks and torn garments, invaded the room. Some bore in their hands a banner with a strange device; many carried goose quills dripping with ink, others clutched musical instruments in their frenzied fingers, whilst many again held palettes and paint brushes in their palsied hands. All strained their eyes and arms towards the vision of the prince.

"He is ours! he is ours! he is ours!" they cried.

"No," said the boarding-house fairy, "he is mine. Were you to take him away, you would all be rich, and then I'd starve to death."

"He is ours! he is ours!" they cried again.

"He belongs to me," said Beatrice.

"I don't wish to quarrel," said Jessie, "but I think he is mine."

"Who," asked the rat, "who can tell me a rhyme for lager?"

No one spoke.

"Go, go," continued the wise old rat, "go back to your dens. Are you presumptuous enough to claim the prince, and you know no rhyme for lager?"

"I can write with lager," said one.

"I can paint with lager," said another.

"I can be brave with lager," cried a third.

"I can swim in lager," sobbed a fourth.

"Yes," said the rat, "but you cannot rhyme with lager."

With despondent mien and drooping heads the boarders shuffled from the room. The prince was alone with Beatrice and Jessie and the rat.

"What will you do now?" asked the rat. "Let me advise you to go home and mend your gowns."

"Never!" said Beatrice. "I won't go home without the prince."

"Nor I," said Jessie; and they made so sudden and violent an onslaught on the exalted one, that, torn by their unruly hands, he fell apart and shed from his gaping wounds a very mound of sawdust.

Beatrice and Jessie stared with open-eyed horror at the sight. At their feet lay a doll, shrunken, broken, and crushed. The rat chuckled. The boarding-house fairy entered with a pitcher of beer. Seeing the prince prone upon the floor, she tenderly raised him, and, sitting down with his poor torn figure across her knee, searched her work-basket for a needle and thread. The rat chuckled again.

Looking out of the window, and lightly strumming with his fingers on the window-pane, he softly hummed:

> "Then when the witch enters
>   To serve the zwei lager,
> You may cut short my tail,
>   For 'tis but a —"

The old rat said no more; he fell over gently, and rendered up his ghost.

Beatrice and Jessie backed slowly towards the door, their thumbs in their mouths, their little under lips quivering. their eyes streaming with tears.

There was a heavy dull thud of silence.

And now I've talked quite enough non-sense, and, moreover, it's time for you children to have your bath.

THE END.

www.ingramcontent.com/pod-product-compliance
Lightning Source LLC
Chambersburg PA
CBHW020538270326
41927CB00006B/636

* 9 7 8 3 7 4 4 6 7 3 5 1 8 *